Contents

To J.D.

Hot Dogs and Cocktails

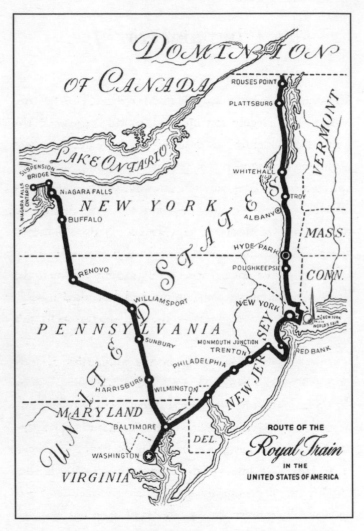

Map of the British royal couple's tour of America in June 1939

Introduction

Winston Churchill's speech in March 1946 in Fulton, Missouri, is largely remembered for his coining of the term "Iron Curtain" to describe the fault line that was beginning to emerge in Europe between the capitalist West and communist East, a divide that was to shape the history of the Continent – and of the world – during the second half of the twentieth century. The speech also contained another phrase that was to have an enduring resonance: Churchill called for a "special relationship between the British Commonwealth and Empire and the United States", which should "work together at the common task as friends and partners".

At the time Churchill spoke, such a relationship already existed. Indeed, it had been displayed to dramatic effect by the US forces that had just stood alongside their British and Commonwealth counterparts on the battlefields of Europe and beyond – as they had done during the First World War. Historians may differ on the moment when the relationship began, but an important stage in its development was undoubtedly represented by a series of meetings between King George VI and Franklin D. Roosevelt at Washington and at the President's family seat at Hyde Park in New York State in June 1939, which form the subject of this book.

I touched briefly on this visit in a previous work, *The King's Speech: How One Man Saved the British Monarchy* (co-written with Mark Logue), which told the true story of the events depicted in the multi-Oscar winning film of the same name. My inspiration to return to it came from another film, *Hyde Park on Hudson*, which has at its heart a picnic that Roosevelt, accompanied by his long-suffering wife, Eleanor, and his domineering mother, Sara, held for the King and Queen Elizabeth at Hyde Park during the visit.

The events of that summer day are little remembered today, but at the time the picnic – and the bizarre question that loomed over it: would or would not the King eat a hot dog? – made headlines on both sides of the Atlantic. Yet the goings-on at Hyde Park were but a small part of a three-week tour of North America that took the royal couple across Canada and back, as well as to New York and Washington.

This was arguably the most important tour in British royal history. For the people of Canada, it was the first time a reigning monarch – *their* monarch – had visited their country. The visit's importance to Britain's ties with America was even greater. It is difficult now, looking back on the close links that have grown up between London and Washington over the past decades, to remember the degree of mutual distrust that still existed between the two countries during the 1930s. The personal relationship between King and President that began at Hyde Park played an important role in turning this distrust into enduring friendship.

In this book, I tell the story of the tour, describing the royal couple's progress across North America and the tumultuous and enthusiastic welcome they received at every point, and setting it in the context of Britain's relations with the United States and with Canada. I also describe the main characters: the King and Queen and the Roosevelts, of course, but also the principal women in the President's life: Margaret "Daisy" Suckley, Marguerite "Missy" LeHand and Lucy Mercer.

The bulk of the narrative has come from the many detailed contemporary newspaper reports of the journey. Also invaluable were two "instant" books: *Voyage of State* by G. Gordon Young, a correspondent for the Reuters news agency who covered the tour, and *North America Sees Our King and Queen* by Keith V. Gordon. The diaries of William Lyon Mackenzie King, who accompanied the royal couple, provided an insider's view of the visit, including near verbatim accounts of some of his conversations with the King, while Eleanor Roosevelt's many writings, together with books by her sons, James and Elliott, gave a wonderful insight into goings-on within the White House that would be unimaginable today.

Among more recent works, *Closest Companion*, edited and annotated by Geoffrey C. Ward, is a fascinating collection of the diaries of Suckley and of her letters to and from Roosevelt, *Franklin and Lucy* by Joseph E. Persico is a masterful study of Roosevelt's love life, while *The Roosevelts and the Royals* by Will Swift charts well the relationship between these two "royal" families.

Chapter 1

Hyde Park on Hudson

No one could remember when they had last flown the Union Jack in Hyde Park, Dutchess County, but the chances were it had been back in colonial times. Now, all those years later, the British flag and the Stars and Stripes were strung in alternate rows between the trees along a short stretch of Main Street. There was a large welcome sign on the approach to the village from the town of Poughkeepsie and smaller ones on several other buildings. The post office, immediately opposite the village garage, strewn with bunting, looked especially festive.

Although home to just eight hundred people, Hyde Park had grown accustomed to its unlikely role as summer capital of the United States. Whenever the opportunity arose, the town's most famous son, Franklin Delano Roosevelt, often known simply as FDR, would slip away from the stresses of Washington DC and pitch up at Springwood, the colonial-style clapboard house set in 1,300 acres of woodland with glorious views of the valley leading down to the Hudson River, which had been in the family for more than seventy years.

Since Roosevelt's election as president almost seven years earlier, this was where he had entertained visiting princes, prime ministers and presidents. Like American leaders before and after him, Roosevelt appreciated the usefulness of a place away from the formality of the White House to which he could invite allies or opponents and pursue politics and diplomacy in a beautiful, relaxed setting. He also loved this house and this particular corner of New York State. It was in his blood. "All that is within me cries out to go back to my home on the Hudson River," he once declared.

It was also where he played, enjoying the company of the various women who had assumed a special role in his life since an affair two decades earlier that had taken the passion out of his marriage to Eleanor, turning their relationship into one of friendship and mutual support. And it was into the surrounding countryside that he would go careering off in his open 1936 Ford Phaeton, which was custom-built with special hand controls that allowed him to drive it without using his feet. Usually, one of those women, maybe Marguerite "Missy" LeHand, his long-serving secretary, or Margaret "Daisy" Suckley, a distant cousin, would be by his side.

Yet the visit this weekend was to be something different: on the evening of Saturday 10th June 1939, Springwood would play host to the King and Queen of the United Kingdom. As the *New York Times* put it, Hyde Park was preparing for a "new and unique role in its history – to serve for one brief weekend as the unofficial capital of the entire English-speaking world".[1]

As citizens of a nation born of a struggle against an earlier British monarch, the people of the United States could have been forgiven a feeling of indifference towards George III's great-great-great-grandson, a quiet and tongue-tied man of forty-four who owed his place on the throne to the decision of his elder brother, Edward VIII, to give up his crown to marry Wallis Simpson.

Nothing could have been further from the truth. Since King George VI and Queen Elizabeth had arrived in Canada just over three weeks earlier, the US newspapers, radio and newsreels had recorded their progress across North America with a growing sense of frenzy. The Americans had been led to expect an uncomfortable, stuttering monarch obsessed with formality and protocol. Instead they encountered a smiling and relaxed man who seemed in many ways just like them – and beside him a charming young woman who dazzled everywhere she went with her beauty and style.

This frenzy had reached a crescendo three days earlier, when the *Royal Blue* train on which they had been travelling through Canada crossed Niagara Falls and they set foot on American soil – making George VI the first reigning British monarch to do so. Their visits to Washington and New York had drawn crowds of more than a million people, more even than had turned out to see them during their many stops north of the border. Now, after a short drive through a part of the United States that had seen some of the fiercest fighting during the war waged by the American colonies against the British Crown, they were due to arrive in Hyde Park.

The locals had initially been slow to latch on to the significance of the occasion, not least when it came to decorating their town. The Town Board had no power to appropriate money for official decorations except on Memorial Day, which had already passed. After much thought, the problem was solved by Elmer Van Wagner, the Hyde Park supervisor, who asked the seven members of the board to stump up $5 each and appealed to village merchants to pay their bit, too. In total, some $80 had been spent on decorations, Van Wagner told the *New York Times*: most of the flags had been rented and a special welcome sign had been made to order at a cost of $4; a special large Union Jack for display in the Town Hall had set them back $4.50.

Asked what he would do with the flag after the visit, Van Wagner paused. "I don't know," he said. "Guess I'll present it to the King." In total, some five to ten thousand people were expected to crowd into the town for the occasion; fields and side streets were to be converted into parking lots to accommodate the influx of cars.

The paper's reporter found the people of Hyde Park taking things in their stride. "While not of the temperament that gives much outward expression to enthusiasm, the inhabitants of this community are giving every indication that they are aware of the role that history has assigned to them for the weekend," he wrote.[2]

So, too, was Roosevelt. Unlikely as it may seem, given the radical nature of his politics, the Democrat President had been brought up with a strong interest in monarchy. As his son, Elliott, wrote later: "He was fascinated by kings and queens, half amused, half impressed by the pomp and pageantry that enveloped royalty."[3] This was due in large part to Roosevelt's mother, Sara, by then a grand old lady of eighty-four, but no less domineering and imperious than she had always been. Sara's own obsession with royalty has been traced back to 1866 when, visiting Paris at the age of twelve, she watched as Empress Eugénie drove past her in the royal coach. Many years later, Sara's husband, James, bought her as a present the red velvet-lined sleigh that Tsar Alexander II had given to Eugénie's husband, Emperor Napoleon III. Sara used it to ride around Springwood during the winter.[4]

In July 1918, when he was a thirty-six-year-old assistant secretary of the Navy, Roosevelt had fulfilled his mother's dream and, during a visit to Europe, was invited to Buckingham Palace to meet King George V. Theodore Roosevelt, a distant cousin, had become a friend of the royal family while he was president before the First World War, and what was meant to have been a formal meeting to discuss the war effort assumed a more personal character. Conversation quickly turned to the twin passions shared by the King and Roosevelt: the Navy and collecting stamps.

And so, two decades later, in the run-up to the royal visit, despite the many other pressing political, economic and military problems facing him, Roosevelt had thrown himself into the organization of the trip and, in particular, the twenty-four hours that the King and Queen would spend at Springwood. From seating plans to choice of furniture and gifts, no detail was too small for the President's attention. Eleanor, although no lover of pomp or formality, had no alternative but to get caught up in the preparations too.

For newspapers on both sides of the Atlantic, though, one small detail of the arrangements mattered more than anything else: would the King and Queen be served hot dogs during the picnic that their hosts planned to hold for them? Since Eleanor had dropped a casual mention of the proposed menu into a press conference a few weeks earlier, the question had assumed almost an iconic importance. There was no better culinary symbol of American classlessness than the humble hot dog. The idea of feeding it to royalty amused and appalled in equal measure – especially after Sara, who never shied away from a public spat with her daughter-in-law, made clear her horror at the very idea of such a "vulgar" food being presented to the King and Queen.

Roosevelt's mind was necessarily on weightier matters. The royal visit came at a sensitive time both for America and for Britain: the future of freedom in Europe was in doubt as Hitler's aggression pushed the Continent towards war.

Roosevelt cared deeply about maintaining that freedom, for the sake of both Europe and the United States. Yet he found himself in a difficult position: many Americans remained deeply suspicious of the Europeans and the British in particular, despite a shared language and culture. Deep-rooted animosity dating back to the War of Independence had been fuelled in recent years by anger at Britain's failure to pay back all its debts from the First World War and by the policy of appeasement that Neville Chamberlain, the Prime Minister, pursued towards Hitler. Whatever the rights and wrongs, many ordinary Americans simply wanted to keep out of an impending conflict thousands of miles away from home.

But the President's hands were tied: although he was personally keen that the United States should play a part in the coming struggle – or, at the very least, help Britain and his allies to arm against Hitler and Mussolini – he knew he would have to carry Congress and the American people with him. What better way to enhance the image of the British at such a sensitive time than by hosting a visit by its two most prominent representatives, the King and Queen?

Just after six o'clock that evening, Roosevelt, Eleanor, Sara and their children sat in the library of Springfield waiting for the royal party to arrive. The President had a tray of cocktails ready in front of him. His mother, who was sitting on the other side of the fireplace, looked disapprovingly across at them. The King would much prefer tea, she said. Roosevelt, who, according to his wife, "could be as obstinate as his mother", refused to back down and kept his tray ready.

Finally, at just after eight o'clock, the waiting was over. The sounds of motor cars announced the arrival of the royal party. One of the most extraordinary twenty-four-hour periods in the history of Anglo-American relations was about to begin.

Chapter 2

The King

King George VI was not fond of trips, especially those that involved making many speeches. As a young child, he had developed a debilitating stammer that turned even ordinary conversations into an ordeal. This impediment, which began to manifest itself when he was eight, was only one of many problems that turned his life into what often seemed a constant stream of challenges.

Born on 14th December 1895 at York Cottage, on the Sandringham estate in East Anglia, Albert Frederick Arthur George – or Bertie, as he was known to the family – was the second son of the future George V and a great-grandson of Queen Victoria, then into her fifty-eighth year on the throne. His early life was spartan and typical of English country life in that era. The estate, which spanned twenty thousand acres, had been bought by his grandfather, the future Edward VII, in 1866 as a shooting retreat. The cottage, given to his father and mother, Mary, was a modest place, situated a few hundred yards from the main house on a grassy mound, built by Edward as overflow accommodation for shooting parties. "The first thing that strikes a visitor about the house itself is its smallness and ugliness," wrote Sarah Bradford, the royal biographer.[1] It was also extremely cramped, becoming home not just to the couple and what were eventually to be their six children, but also to a number of staff.

Like other English upper-class children of the day, Bertie and his siblings had only a distant relationship with their parents. What contact he had with his father was often harsh. An unbending Victorian who had spent his formative years in the Navy, the future George V believed in inculcating a strict sense of discipline from an early age – as was clear from a letter he wrote to his son on his fifth birthday. "Now that you are five years old I hope you will always try & be obedient & do at once what you are told, as you will find it much easier to you the sooner you begin. I always tried to do this when I was your age & found it made me much happier," he wrote.[2] Punishment for transgressions was administered in the library – which, despite its name, was largely devoid of books and filled instead with George V's stamp collection, to which he devoted his leisure time when he was not taken up with his other pursuits of shooting and sailing. The room was remembered by his children as a "place of admonishment and reproof".[3]

Bertie was a sickly boy: suffering from an early age from poor digestion, he had to wear splints on his legs for many hours of the day and at night to cure him of the knock knees from which his father suffered. He was also left-handed, but, according to the practice of the day, obliged to write with his right hand. Furthermore, he was constantly in the shadow of his elder brother, David, the future Edward VIII. Just eighteen months older, David was good-looking, charming and fun – and destined one day to become king. The two were inevitably close, but it was an unequal relationship: "When we were young, I could always manage him," David wrote years later in his autobiography.[4]

It is difficult to pinpoint the cause of Bertie's stammer, but it was certainly exacerbated by the attitude of his father, whose response to his son's struggles could be summed up with a simple phrase: "Just get it out." The stammer proved to be a problem at the Royal Naval College, based at Queen Victoria's former residence Osborne House on the Isle of Wight, where he and his elder brother were sent for their education. Although good at practical subjects such as engineering and seamanship, Bertie was poor at mathematics, often coming near the bottom of the class. His problems were compounded by his stammer: on one occasion, he failed to respond when asked what was a half of a half because he was unable to pronounce the initial consonant of "quarter" – which produced an unfortunate reputation for stupidity. In the final examination, held in December 1910, he came sixty-eighth out of sixty-eight.

On 15th September 1913, aged seventeen, he began his naval career, after he was commissioned as a junior midshipman on the battleship HMS *Collingwood*. Like his father before him, he expected this to be his life for the next few years. Although he worshipped the Navy as an institution, he did not much like the sea itself – and was plagued with seasickness. He was also shy. One fellow officer, Lieutenant F.J. Lambert, described the Prince as a "small, red-faced youth with a stutter", adding: "When he reported his boat to me he gave a story of stutter and an explosion. I had no idea who he was and very nearly cursed him for spluttering at me."[5] Proposing a toast to his father, who had become king in 1910, was a torment because of the initial "k" sound.

Days before Britain declared war on Germany on 3rd August 1914, *Collingwood* was sent to Scapa Flow in the Orkneys, to guard the northern entrance to the North Sea. Bertie's wartime career was not an especially glorious one, however: after just three weeks he began to experience violent pains in his stomach and suffer difficulty with his breathing; he was diagnosed with appendicitis and sent to Aberdeen for surgery. Although he subsequently returned to his ship and took part in the Battle of Jutland in May 1916, he endured repeated stomach problems that were eventually diagnosed as an ulcer. By July 1917, ill once more and transferred ashore to a hospital near Edinburgh, he reluctantly accepted that, after eight years of either training or serving in the Navy, his career was over. "Personally, I feel that I am not fit for service at sea, even after I recover from this little attack," he wrote to his father.[6]

Following the end of the war, he returned to civilian life, and after a year at Trinity College, Cambridge, where he studied history, economics and civics, he became drawn into the public side of royal life: he developed a special interest in industrial welfare, visiting coal mines, factories and rail yards; and, in July 1921, instituted a series of annual seaside summer camps designed to bring together boys from different social backgrounds.

Bertie was also beginning to rise in the estimation of his father, who was having misgivings about David and his apparent disregard for duty and tradition and love of the modern – as well as his predilection for married women. On 4th June 1920, aged twenty-four, Bertie became Duke of York, Earl of Inverness and Baron Killarney. "I know that you have behaved very well, in a difficult situation for a young man & that you have done what I asked you to," his father wrote to him. "I hope you will always look upon me as yr. best friend & always tell me everything & you will always find me ever ready to help you and give you good advice."[7]

It was a month later that the Duke met Elizabeth Bowes-Lyon, the daughter of the 14th Earl of Strathmore and Kinghorne, a society beauty five years his junior. He spotted her across a crowded room at a ball, asked her to dance and soon decided she was the only woman for him. Two proposals of marriage followed – both of which she rejected. "I honestly can't explain to you how terribly sorry I am – it worries me so much to think you may be unhappy," she wrote to him on 28th February 1921. "Anyway we can be good friends can't we? I shall never say anything about our talks I promise you – and nobody need ever know."[8] The Duke persisted, however, and she accepted on his third attempt. They married on 26th April 1923 in Westminster Abbey, the first time it had been used for a royal wedding.

Marriage proved a turning point; happier and more at ease with himself, the Duke became far more confident. Public speaking nevertheless remained an ordeal, despite the considerable support his wife provided him. A low point was reached in May 1925, when the Duke was due to succeed his elder brother as president of the Empire Exhibition in Wembley. The previous year David had made a speech formally asking his father for permission to open the event, a massive festival that was to draw some twenty million visitors. In a first, the Prince's words and his father's response had been broadcast to the world by the British Broadcasting Company (later Corporation). "Everything went off most successfully," the King noted in his diary.[9]

It was now the Duke's turn. He had only a few words to say, which he practised intensely, but his dread of public speaking was such that the whole thing turned into a terrifying ordeal – even more so because for the first time he was speaking in front of his father. The speech, broadcast not just in Britain but around the world, ended in humiliation. Although through sheer determination he managed to reach the end, there were embarrassing moments when his jaw muscle moved frantically and no sound came out. The King tried to put a positive gloss on it. "Bertie got through his speech all right, but there were some long pauses," he wrote to the Duke's young brother, Prince George, the following day.[10]

It would be difficult to overestimate the psychological effect that the speech had on both the Duke and his family, and the problem that his faltering performance created for the monarchy, for which such performances were a part of daily routine. As one contemporary biographer put it, "it was becoming increasingly manifest that very drastic steps would have to be taken if he were not to develop into the shy retiring nervous individual which is the common fate of all those suffering from speech defects".[11]

There was a need to take such steps urgently: the Duke and Duchess were due to embark in January 1927 on a six-month trip to Australia and New Zealand that would be full of speaking engagements the high point of it on 9th May when he was due to open the new Commonwealth Parliament House in Canberra. The *Daily Telegraph* claimed the speech he would make there would be as historic as the proclamation of Queen Victoria as Empress of India in 1877. With all eyes – and ears – upon him, Bertie could not risk a repetition of the Wembley fiasco.

It was this that led the Duke, with some prompting from his wife, to draw on the services of Lionel Logue, a charismatic elocution teacher turned speech therapist who opened a practice on Harley Street after arriving from his native Australia in 1924. During their first consultation on 19th October 1926, Logue heard the Duke's problems, in particular with the hard "k" sound – as in "king" – and established he had "an acute nervous tension brought on by the defect". He diagnosed the underlying problem, as with many of his patients, as one of faulty breathing. Logue prescribed an hour of concentrated effort, made up of breathing exercises of his own invention, coupled with gargling with warm water and standing in front of a window, intoning the vowels one by one, each for fifteen seconds. "I can cure you," Logue declared at the end of the session, which lasted for an hour and a half, "but it will need a tremendous effort by you. Without that effort, it can't be done."[12]

The Duke made considerable progress, thanks to intensive consultations – some eighty-two of them during the fourteen months leading up to his departure for Australia. Though lacking the easy fluency of his elder brother, he made a success of his speeches in Australia – even the all-important one in Canberra. "I have so much more confidence in myself now, which I am sure comes from being able to speak properly at last," the Duke wrote in a letter to his father.[13] He continued to consult Logue after his return, but their meetings became less frequent; after one consultation in March 1932 they did not meet again for almost two years. Although the King's age and deteriorating health meant more duties for him and his brother, he proved to be up to the task.

The Duke's life was to be transformed by the events of 1936, "the year of three kings". On the evening of 15th January, the elderly George V took to his bed, complaining of a cold. He died shortly afterwards, his final passing hastened by a lethal injection of cocaine and morphine, administered by Lord Dawson of Penn, his physician.

David, who succeeded him as Edward VIII, came to the throne with huge accumulated goodwill: with his radiant good looks, love of the modern and avowed concern for the ordinary man (or woman), he seemed to embody the new age. His reign was to last just 327 days, however: forced to choose between the throne and Wallis Simpson, an American divorcee, he abdicated on 10th December, declaring in a broadcast to the nation from Windsor Castle: "I have found it impossible to carry on the heavy burden of responsibility and to discharge the duties of king as I would wish to do without the help and support of the woman I love."

The Duke, who took his brother's place as King George VI, grew into the role that had been thrust upon him. His stammer continued to weigh on him, however, and, in the run-up to his coronation the following May, he re-established contact with his speech therapist. He and Logue spent several weeks preparing the responses he would have to make in Westminster Abbey and, more terrifying, the broadcast to the people of Britain and the Empire he was due to make the same evening.

The King's big day went well. "Slow, deliberate and clear, his voice betrayed no sign of fatigue," commented the *Daily Telegraph*. Those listening outside Britain to the King's performance wondered what had become of the speech impediment they had heard so much about. "It wasn't apparent throughout the entire ceremony, and after hearing the new king deliver his address, many persons are classifying him with President Roosevelt as possessing a perfect radio voice," wrote the compiler of the *Detroit Free Press*'s radio notes.[14] Many more speeches and broadcasts were to follow; yet, despite the progress he continued to make, the King was never completely comfortable in front of a microphone or a crowd.

Chapter 3

Planning the Trip

The idea for a royal visit to North America had been suggested in the run-up to George VI's coronation by Lord Tweedsmuir, the Canadian Governor General, better known as the writer John Buchan, whose more than eighty books included the suspense novel *The Thirty-Nine Steps*. Tweedsmuir pushed the visit hard, and when William Lyon Mackenzie King, the Canadian Prime Minister, visited London for the ceremony, he gave the King and Queen a personal invitation. Mackenzie King had tipped off Roosevelt, and he, in turn, instructed his special envoy, James Gerard, who represented him at the coronation, to suggest to the King that if he went to Canada he should visit the United States too. The King told Gerard he would be delighted to do so.

For Roosevelt the idea of welcoming the British monarch to America, even if only briefly, had considerable attractions. The presence of the royal couple would, he hoped, further his aim of winning popular support among Americans for closer relations with a Britain that seemed one of the few defences against Nazi Germany. Eleanor was in no doubt as to the President's motivation. "My husband invited them to Washington largely because, believing that we all might soon be engaged in a life-and-death struggle, in which Great Britain would be our first line of defence, he hoped that their visit would create a bond of friendship between the people of the two countries," she wrote later. "He knew that, although there is always in this country a certain amount of criticism and superficial ill feeling toward the British, in time of danger something deeper comes to the surface, and the British and we stand firmly together, with confidence in our common heritage and ideas. The visit of the King and Queen, he hoped, would be a reminder of this deep bond."[1]

There was also a tinge of snobbery: in protocol terms, George VI, King of the United Kingdom and Emperor of India, was rivalled only by Roosevelt himself, and perhaps the Pope. As one of the President's biographers put it, "Roosevelt the descendant of Yankee merchants, Roosevelt the Hudson Valley squire, Roosevelt the politician disparaged by much of America's ostensible aristocracy for his reformist policies could not fail to find the potentialities of such a visit interesting, even piquant."[2]

For Britain, the motivation was even clearer. War was coming to Europe, and the British government was searching for allies. Canada, like other members of the Empire, was duty-bound to support the British, but the United States was a different matter. Despite the shared language, Anglo-American relations in the 1930s were not as cordial as they were to become in the second half of the twentieth century. True, both sides had moved on since the War of American Independence and the Anglo-American war of 1812–15, during which British forces occupied Washington and burned down the White House. Cultural ties between the two great English-speaking nations remained close, and America had sided with Britain against Germany in the First World War.

Yet sympathy for the British was far from universal. For many, the country still represented the snobbishness and class consciousness that they had come to America to escape. The British Empire was not just a potential competitor for the United States but also, in the eyes of many liberals, an anachronism. Irish, Italian or Jewish Americans could not be expected to feel the same natural sympathy for Britain as those whose ancestors had come over on the *Mayflower*. The abdication crisis and the disdain shown by the British establishment towards Wallis Simpson – inspired as much, it seemed, by the fact she was an American as that she was a divorcee – was also perceived by many as a snub.

American memories of the First World War were furthermore tinged with bitterness; in one poll in January 1937, seventy per cent of Americans said it had been a mistake to take part in the conflict. There was little enthusiasm for the idea of being drawn into another. This was not just because of the inevitable suffering and loss of life. There was concern, too, about the implications of total war and full-scale mobilization. For many conservatives, this would lead to inflation and controls on wages and prices – in short, the creation of a form of wartime socialism that would endure beyond the end of the conflict. "God knows what will happen here before we finish it [the Second World War] – race riots, revolution, destruction," declared Colonel Charles A. Lindbergh, the aviator who became one of the leading members of the anti-war movement after his return from self-imposed exile in Europe in April 1939. Liberal isolationists drew the opposite conclusion: total war would engulf the country in "armament economics" and risk turning the clock back to the days of President Calvin Coolidge, when big business was triumphant.

Despite growing horror at Hitler's actions at home and abroad, many Americans believed that Britain and France shared responsibility for his rise to power as a result of the punitive conditions they had imposed on Germany at Versailles after the First World War. There was also widespread anger that Britain had still not repaid its debts from the war. Add fears of the communist peril, which to some seemed a greater danger than that posed by Hitler, and it was understandable why there was reluctance to become involved. Resistance was especially strong in the Midwest, where the *Chicago Tribune*, under its owner, Robert Rutherford McCormick, was a bastion of isolationism. It was no coincidence that many of the people who lived there had their origins in mainland Europe rather than in Britain.

In the mid-1930s, as the international situation deteriorated and American isolationism grew, the British government began a concerted campaign to improve its standing in the United States. An important role was played by Ronald Lindsay, who had become ambassador in 1930. Based in Washington on and off since 1905 and having had two American wives – the first the daughter of a senator and the second, Elizabeth Hoyt Lindsay, a long-time friend of Eleanor Roosevelt – Lindsay knew well the country to which he was posted. He also understood that it was as important to work on American public opinion as on the government itself. As he told Anthony Eden, the Foreign Secretary, "I hold that East and West and even the middle can be worked on through emotions. The late King George broadcasting to his Empire, Mr Baldwin's speech in the House on the abdication crisis, the Stratford Shakespeare Company, *Goodbye, Mr Chips* by Hilton, Noël Coward's film *Cavalcade*, the successes of Great Britain, the calmness and the dignity of their people, these are the things that move America."[3]

The royal visit could be understood in this context. For Britain, it would be an opportunity to emphasize the many things that united rather than divided the two countries, drawing a line under what, almost two centuries earlier, had been the biggest schism in the English-speaking world. Yet London and Washington were still a long way from any kind of formal alliance. The isolationist mood in the United States was reflected in Congress and had found its legislative expression in the Neutrality Acts, a series of laws passed in the mid-1930s aimed at keeping the country out of any further European entanglements. Roosevelt and Cordell Hull, his secretary of state, were critical of the laws, fearing they would restrict the administration's options when it came to supporting America's allies. Yet, although the President could have used his veto against them, he had been reluctant to do so in the run-up to his re-election bid in 1936.

In a concession the following year, a so-called "cash and carry" provision was added to the law that would allow the President to permit the sale of materials and supplies to belligerents in Europe provided they were paid for immediately in cash and not carried in American ships – the idea being that if the ship were sunk or the cargo seized, the United States would not be drawn into any conflict. The provision was set to expire after two years on 1st May 1939 but, although Roosevelt lobbied to have it renewed, he did not succeed.

A confidential briefing document drawn up for the King by Ronald Lindsay ahead of his visit provides an intriguing insight into how Anglo-American relations looked from the British side. Sympathy in America for Britain had grown markedly, the report argued, not just because of shared fears about Germany, but also because of the naval and trade agreements concluded by the two countries and the establishment of the Irish Free State in 1922, which had removed a long-standing grievance in the United States. That being said, Americans failed to understand why Britain had not stood up more to Hitler and Mussolini over Abyssinia and at Munich – even if relations had improved as a result of the harder line London had pursued in the months since.

"There is still a good deal of distrust and suspicion that we 'we may rat again'," the report commented. "The fact is that the more forcefully we stand up to the Dictators, the more we will be applauded by the United States, though by and large the latter will not give too much thought to the state of our armaments. And from the very nature of things the United States can never pledge its action in advance for any contingency." This was all the more problematic, the report added, since "nearly everyone in America wants to stay neutral if a war comes" – a position that had been reflected in the various Neutrality Acts passed by Congress.[4]

It was against this complicated backdrop that preparations for the royal visit continued. The date was originally set for 1939, but the crisis over Czechoslovakia that erupted in the summer of 1938 meant that the King and his advisor began to doubt whether it would be wise to go ahead. Tweedsmuir was lobbying hard, however, arguing that the trip should take place unless the international situation took a sharp turn for the worse. As he told his sister: "I pressed it with the persistence of a horseleech. As soon as I got Neville

[Chamberlain] on my side I knew it would be all right, for the King was most sympathetic."[5]

The trip's advocates could also cite the positive example of the four-day state visit that the King and Queen had paid that July to France. Several months in the making, the trip – the first by the monarch outside Britain since he came to the throne – had been intended both to strengthen relations between France and Britain and, in its style, to underline the contrast between the liberal democracies and the dictatorships of Germany and Italy. Comparisons were inevitably drawn with the visit by the King's grandfather, Edward VII, to Paris in 1903, which had led to the establishment of the Entente Cordiale. At that time, the French had feared the rise of a Germany armed to the teeth under Kaiser Wilhelm II. Just over three decades later, the French were again worried about German militarism; this visit was intended to underline the continued importance to both sides of the Entente.

"I think the Paris visit would have an excellent effect internally and all classes would vie with one another in giving Their Majesties an enthusiastic reception," declared Sir Eric Phipps, the British ambassador to Paris, earlier that year. "Externally it seems clear that the visit would produce a most healthy effect upon Hitler, Mussolini and Co., who like to think that the streets of Paris are running in blood or at any rate very dangerous to walk about in."[6]

The British were not to be disappointed. The King and Queen were greeted with a great military display – the greatest since the Armistice parade after the First World War – as they arrived at the Bois de Boulogne station aboard a special train that had brought them from the coast. A 101-gun royal salute rang out as they pulled into the station. The President, Albert Lebrun, accompanied by his wife and members of the Cabinet, were waiting to receive them. Two hours before their arrival, the army virtually took over the city: tanks rolled through the boulevards, taking up commanding positions in the Place de la Concorde and the Champs-Élysées, barring all traffic. Some thirty-five thousand troops were stationed along the route from the station to the Quai d'Orsay, where the royal couple stayed in the state apartments of the Foreign Office, which had been refurnished and redecorated since George V and Queen Mary had visited in 1919.

The French were flattered that the King had chosen to visit their country before travelling to one of the Dominions. The trip had to be postponed for three weeks because of the death of the Queen's mother, the Countess of Strathmore, but the delay seemed only to add to the sense of feverish anticipation. Huge crowds turned out to greet the royal couple, whose programme included visits to the Louvre, the opera and Versailles as well as to the unveiling of the Australian national war memorial at Villers-Bretonneux near Amiens: almost every window in the centre of Paris was decorated with the Union Jack, and buses were decked with French and British flags. A special stamp was produced showing two hands clasping each other across the Channel, with the Houses of Parliament and the Arc de Triomphe between them. Newspapers on both sides of the Channel brought out special editions.

There had been speculation in the British press that the King might take advantage of his presence in Paris to pay a visit to the Duke of Windsor, who had taken a lease on the Château de la Maye in Versailles. "There can be no reason why not," said the *Daily Express* in an editorial. "There are good reasons why they should meet. The King and the brother who was king have no quarrel. The episode of December 1936 is closed for ever."[7] It was not to be; the King refused his elder brother's request to see him, describing a state visit as "a most unsuitable moment" for a meeting and urged him to leave town while he was there. The Duke, deeply slighted, reluctantly agreed to do so, but only on condition that he be invited to the British embassy for a formal reception before the visit. The King conceded but insisted that the event not be publicized; his brother responded by leaking it to the press.

This latest instalment in the battle between the two brothers did not detract from the success of the trip, which was seen as a personal triumph – not just for the tongue-tied King, but also for the Queen, whose wardrobe in "mourning white" (the accepted alternative to black), specially designed for the occasion by her favourite couturier, Norman Hartnell, went down especially well with the French.

The pair's presence also appeared to have breathed new life into Anglo-French relations, fuelling hopes that Europe's two most powerful democracies would unite and seize the initiative from the totalitarian regimes that had dominated the Continent over the previous few years. Leslie Hore-Belisha, the British war minister, declared that the two countries were united under "what seems to be one general staff and one flag". Georges Bonnet, the French foreign minister, said it was "impossible to recall a period when relations have been more intimate".

The message was taken up by commentators elsewhere too. "The political partnership between Great Britain and France which was formally celebrated by the King and Queen's visit to Paris this week is far closer than the entente to which George VI's grandfather [Edward VII] was credited with contributing thirty-four years ago," concluded the *New York Times* at the end of the trip.[8] Sadly, such euphoria rapidly faded in the face of yet more German aggression.

And so, with the success of the French visit much in mind, it was decided to press ahead with the royal trip to North America. When Mackenzie King met Roosevelt on 18th August 1938 for the dedication of the International Bridge at the Thousand Islands, linking northern New York with south-eastern Ontario, he told the American President

that the King would in all likelihood pay a visit the following year.

On 17th September, Roosevelt sat down to write what was
to be the first personal letter from an American president to
a British sovereign.[9] The tone was friendly and surprisingly
informal. Roosevelt said he had been told in confidence by
Mackenzie King of the King's impending tour and suggested
he add a few days in the United States. "I need not assure
you that it would give my wife and me the greatest pleasure to see you and, frankly, I think it would be an excellent
thing for Anglo-American relations if you could visit the
United States," he wrote. "I have had, as you know, the great
privilege of knowing your splendid Father, and I have also
known two of your brothers. Therefore, I am greatly looking
forward to the possibility of meeting you and the Queen."

The President's initial proposal was that the tour should be
as much as possible an informal and private one, rather than a
grand state occasion. At its heart would be "three or four days
of very simple country life at Hyde Park". The royal couple
could also perhaps visit the World's Fair due to be held in New
York in 1939, but there would be "no formal entertainment
and an opportunity to get a bit of rest and relaxation". If,
however, the King wanted to add Washington to his itinerary,
then the whole visit would necessarily have to be more formal.

"You and I are fully aware of the demands of the Protocol
people, but, having had much experience with them, I am
inclined to think that you and Her Majesty should do very

much as you personally want to do – and I will see to it over here that your decision becomes the right decision," the President wrote. He ended on an especially informal note: "I forgot to mention that if you bring either or both of the children with you, they will also be very welcome, and I shall try to have one or two Roosevelts of approximately the same age to play with them."

As the President made clear in the letter, he was keen to keep any discussion of the visit out of the usual diplomatic channels. So he passed the invitation to Joseph Kennedy, whom he had sent as US ambassador to London that January, and noted that Lindsay, his British opposite number, was a very old and close personal friend.

The letter was received at the height of the Munich crisis. On 12th September 1938, during a mass rally in Nuremberg, Hitler had demanded justice for the three million German speakers in Czechoslovakia and, after stirring up clashes between them and the Czechs in which he claimed erroneously that three hundred Germans had been killed, he placed troops along the Czech border. Although Britain and France had given a guarantee to the government in Prague, neither country was ready to intervene in what Chamberlain described as "a quarrel in a faraway country between people of whom we know nothing". And so, three days later, Chamberlain flew to Munich and then on to Hitler's mountain retreat at Berchtesgaden, starting a process that was to culminate in the early hours of 30th

September in the high point of appeasement: the signature of the Munich Agreement, which allowed Germany to annexe the Sudetenland.

On his return to Britain later that day, Chamberlain waved to the cheering crowds who met him at the airport a short declaration by Hitler and him that the agreement they had signed in Munich was "symbolic of the desire of our two people never to go to war again". In words that would subsequently haunt him, the Prime Minister declared: "I believe it is peace for our time. We thank you from the bottom of our hearts. And now I recommend you to go home and sleep quietly in your beds."

The King, who had travelled down from Balmoral to London to attend the funeral of his cousin, Prince Arthur of Connaught, had been embroiled in the crisis, consulting with Chamberlain and other members of the Cabinet, and even proposing that he should make his own personal appeal to Hitler. His offer was declined. And when Chamberlain came back from Munich, the King invited the Prime Minister and his wife to join him and the Queen on the balcony of Buckingham Palace to receive the plaudits of the crowds below who believed in his claim to have secured "peace with honour".

It was therefore not until 8th October, when the King had resumed his interrupted holiday and was back at Balmoral, that he was finally able to reply to Roosevelt. His tone was equally cordial. "Your letter, which Mr Kennedy handed to me last week, came as a pleasant relief at a time of great anxiety, and I thank you warmly for it," the King wrote. But while welcoming the invitation both for the pleasure it would give personally and the contribution it would make to "the cordiality of relations" between the two countries, the King said he would not be able to respond until the plans for his visit to Canada were further advanced, which would allow him to judge how long he could be away from Britain. He also politely declined the offer to take along his two daughters – the princesses Elizabeth and Margaret Rose – on the grounds that the visit to Canada would be far too strenuous for them.[10]

Roosevelt was undaunted by this apparent uncertainty, and on 2nd November he sent a letter with some more detailed proposals, which crossed one the following day from the King saying that he and the Queen would indeed be delighted to include in the itinerary of their trip to Canada a four-day visit to the United States that would take in Washington, New York and Hyde Park.

Finalizing the details of the programme was to prompt much discussion. Understandably, given his stammer, the King wanted to avoid major speeches, and so turned down a proposal that he address a special session of both houses of Congress. There was concern on the British side that a suggested visit to the World's Fair in New York City might be seen as a royal endorsement of a commercial venture. A traditional ticker-tape parade of the sort given to visiting celebrities was considered too vulgar for a reigning monarch.

Even more potentially problematic was the Hyde Park leg of the visit. For Roosevelt, the opportunity to host the King and Queen in his family home was one of the main attractions of the trip. British diplomats disagreed. Although not against a visit to the house per se, Ambassador Lindsay warned that any attempt to make Springwood – rather than Washington – the centrepiece could backfire by emphasizing "the personal nature of the visit to the President too much for American opinion".[11]

Lady Reading, whose husband had been his predecessor as ambassador, also weighed into the debate, sneering about the suitability of the main house at Springwood for royal guests. "I believe I am one of the very few English people who have stayed at Hyde Park with the President," she wrote to Lord Halifax, the Foreign Secretary, the following February, "and I must admit it is a dismal small house, extremely badly run and most uncomfortable. I shiver to think of what would happen if the King and Queen went to stay there."[12]

The royal visit to Canada had been announced in a brief statement from Balmoral on 8th October – the same day the King had replied to Roosevelt. But although there was immediate speculation that he and the Queen would also visit the United States, it was not until a month later during his speech opening Parliament that the King declared he would be "happy to accept" the President's invitation, adding: "I welcome this practical expression of the good feeling that prevails between our countries."

The British press were enthusiastic: "History will be made on this occasion," declared the *Daily Mail* in an editorial. "Never before has a British sovereign set foot in North America... They are certain to receive a tumultuous reception from the warm-hearted American people whose reputation for hospitality is world famous." The news was also largely favourably reported in the US media, although the newspapers belonging to the media empire founded by the retired magnate William Randolph Hearst were cool and the isolationist *Chicago Tribune* downright hostile.

When, in the same month, Winston Churchill addressed the American people in a broadcast over the NBC radio network proposing closer Anglo-American ties, Hearst replied over the same network. In his broadcast, translated into five languages, he launched a ferocious attack on "England's invariable selfishness", "perfidy" and "treachery" and accused her of trying to drag America into war. "If England needs help, where should she turn but to good old Uncle Sam, who is so sought after when needed, and so scoffed at in the intervening times," he thundered. "The English soft soap is being poured over Uncle Sam's devoted head and lathered into his ears and eyes."[13]

The announcement of the visit prompted criticism of Britain in Congress too. During a debate in the Senate on national defence in January 1939, Robert Rice Reynolds, the strongly isolationist Democratic senator from North Carolina, launched a fierce attack on the trip. After complaining that America's contribution to winning the First World War was not recognized in France or Britain, who refused to admit that they owed money to Washington, Reynolds voiced displeasure at the prospect of the King and Queen coming to "curry favour with the United States, all of them on bended knee, if not literally so, figuratively so, for the purpose of asking the United States, the people of America, again to save them". Commenting on the speech, the *Baltimore Sun* noted that, in taking issue with royalty, Reynolds "has campaign material of incalculable, noise-making potentiality" and said there seemed no apparent reason why he would not continue his denunciation of royalty indefinitely.[14]

The overwhelming mood in the American papers, however, was enthusiastic. Speculation about what the royal couple would do, where they would go and whom they would meet during their stay had already been building in the weeks leading to the announcement. The style, often tongue-in-cheek, was to characterize much of the coverage in the weeks and months that followed. For the *Milwaukee Journal* there was "at least one very grave question to decide", and that was the seating plan for the inevitable White House dinner: would it follow American rules, according to which the President and his wife would sit opposite each other, with the Queen and King to their respective right-hand sides, or "Buckingham Palace usage", with the President and the King next to each other? The latter method had been used only once before, during a visit by the King and Queen of Siam in 1931, and had caused consternation among veterans of such formal dinners.[15]

And then there was the question of where the royal visitors might stay: "Capital society is disturbed by the problem of where to house a king and queen in Washington," the Associated Press news agency had reported in a story carried in many newspapers on 6th November. "When the King and Queen were in Paris, they were put up in a real palace, and Napoleon's bed was dusted off and brought from a museum for the King, while the Queen was given Marie Antoinette's. With no palaces on hand, tea-table Washington is in a flutter."

As to what the royal couple should do during their trip, the agency harked back to a packed visit, back in October 1919, by Albert the King of the Belgians, who had managed during a brief stay to see Niagara Falls, address former soldiers in Salt Lake City, kiss babies through Iowa and Nebraska, go to both a football game and the opera, christen a ship, lay a wreath on Theodore Roosevelt's tomb and assure America that Belgium would pay all its wartime debts.

As time went on, other questions began to emerge – among them how Americans should react in the royal presence. More particularly, would men be required to bow and women to curtsy? "No," came the answer the following February. And there would be no need for knee pants, silk stockings or court dress either. "Just act natural and democratic," was the message from the State Department, according to one report. "The good old American hand-shake will prevail – with other American customs and dress at functions held for King George and Queen Elizabeth. Without actually saying so, the diplomats indicated they didn't want the visit marred by someone falling flat at the feet of royalty while trying to execute a fancy but unfamiliar knee bend." And importantly, the report went on, "There will be nothing in the visit to indicate the British monarchs are paying a belated call on a former colony. Democracy and democratic practices will prevail."[16]

Talk of the visit also gave the American press an oppor-tunity to revisit the royal family drama that had been triggered by the abdication. A meeting between the Duke of Gloucester, one of George VI's younger brothers, and the exiled Duke and Duchess of Windsor in Paris in November 1938, a few days after the announcement of the trip, was seized upon by the newspapers. It was the first such visit by a member of the royal family since the Duke and Duchess had married in June the previ-ous year and prompted reports of a possible thaw in relations ahead of the royal visit to America. Unnamed friends of the exiled couple speculated the Duke and Duchess might even be invited to spend Christmas with the royal family. It turned out to be little more than wishful thinking.

Two years after the abdication, the former King, according to the Associated Press, was a fading memory. "The wave of emotion of two years ago is scarcely a ripple of mild interest as far as the doings of David Windsor are concerned," it said. "England has almost forgotten him, except when it is reminded once in a while, perhaps because it has had so many other things to worry about." By contrast, respect was growing for his successor, who, as everyone realized, "has worked like a Trojan, overcome physical disadvantages and, above all, behaved himself".[17] The Duke had further blotted his copybook with a visit to Nazi Germany in October 1937, during which he had met Adolf Hitler at his mountain redoubt of Berchtesgaden and even attempted a half-hearted Nazi salute. He had been planning to follow it up with a visit to the United States, but was forced to call it off after hostile stories in the American press and threat of protests by labour unions.

The Duke's problems did not necessarily translate into universal praise for his younger brother, however. Particular consternation in London was caused by a long article in America's *Scribner's Magazine*, published in February 1939 and penned by Josef Israels II, who was described as "a press agent". The article, entitled 'Selling George VI to the US', was written in the form of an imaginary memorandum sent by a public-relations firm to the Foreign Office on how to handle the forthcoming royal trip. "Selling a king and queen of England to the United States is essentially a public-relations job, just as much as it would be to sell a product made in Great Britain," Israels began.[18]

The author made a number of fairly uncontroversial suggestions as to how the royal couple should satisfy what were bound to be the many demands of the American press while attempting to strike a balance between "dignified regal reserve on the one hand and democratic friendliness on the other". Yet he also questioned the quality of the "product" that was being sold to the American public. No public-relations expert with the power to choose from scratch "which British personalities he would drop into the American scene for the greatest British profit" would have gone for either the King or the Queen, Israels argued. "The important fact about public opinion in the United States [...] is that a large part of the country still believes that Edward, Duke of Windsor, is the rightful owner of the British throne, and that King George VI is a color-less, weak personality largely on probation in the public mind of Great Britain, as well as of the United States." As for the Queen, "according to Park Avenue standards, she appears to be far too plump of figure, too dowdy in dress to meet American specifications of a reigning queen", with nothing of the regal bearing of her mother-in-law, Queen Mary, or the chic and American charm of the Duchess of Windsor.

For that reason, Israels suggested that, before leaving for America, the King provide some public evidence of reconciliation with the Duke, inviting him and the Duchess to Buckingham Palace and granting Wallis the title of "Her Royal Highness" – something that the former King had wanted and his younger brother had refused to concede. It might also be a good idea for the King and Queen to find a "graceful method" to make amends for the British burning of the White House – perhaps a house gift of some sort. "It must be borne in mind," Israels added, "that many ignorant Americans, particularly among those of Irish extraction, still believe the English people, and British royalty especially, to be evil intentioned with ambitions to conquer the whole world."

Victor Mallet, a diplomat at the British embassy who sent the article back to London, did so without comment, save to note that "the question of press interviews will be an important one and the suggestions in this article, although inevitably claiming rather too large a share of Their Majesties' time for the press, are not without interest and imagination".[19]

The reaction back at the Foreign Office, by contrast, bordered on fury, judging by handwritten comments on a file containing the piece by Israels. "This article, apparently by a member of some Jewish dynasty, strikes me as a rather unpleasant production," wrote one official, expressing surprise at Mallet's comment. Sir Eric Mieville, the King's assistant private secretary, was downright dismissive. "I understand that the magazine in question has been going downhill for some time, and does not hold the position in the American press world which it had some years ago," he wrote to the Foreign Office.[20] Mieville was right: that May's issue was to be *Scribner's* last. It was decided to ignore the offending article.

Reaction in the press to the views expressed by Israels, meanwhile, was predictably hostile. "George VI is neither colorless nor weak," retorted a London correspondent for the North American Newspaper Alliance. "Far from it. He expresses his views in the most robust language very often and he is full of good sense [...]. Most Britons believe that, if the present King of England lives long enough, he will develop into much the same man as his father George V was – a sound, level-headed sovereign – with a high sense of duty, and with a considerable amount of political influence behind the scenes."[21]

In the meantime, the question of the precise royal itinerary had still to be resolved. In a letter to the King on 18th January 1939, Roosevelt proposed a plan for the US part of the royal visit, which would begin at 9.30 p.m. on Wednesday 7th June, when the royal train arrived on the American side of Niagara Falls, and end with the King and Queen's departure on the Sunday evening. They would start with packed visits to Washington and New York, including a state dinner in the White House on the Thursday evening, and then go on to Hyde Park, where the pace would be slower. "I have tried in arranging these three and a half days to give you and Her Majesty some opportunity for relaxation because I know that your trip to Vancouver will, of necessity, be tiring," the President wrote.[22] The King replied on 8th February, accepting the plan, though with a few suggested minor tweaks including an official dinner to be thrown in honour of Roosevelt at the British embassy on the Friday evening.

Some thought it would be an error to confine the visit to the East Coast and argued that the King and Queen should also fly the flag among the isolationists of the Midwest. The idea was championed by Lady Reading, who passed on to the Foreign Office a letter from her friend, Helen Woods, the niece of "Jack" Morgan, the banker and philanthropist. The East Coast didn't need converting to the cause of greater cooperation with Britain, Woods argued, but the Midwest was quite another matter. Adding Chicago to the royal itinerary "would have the inestimable advantage of making the Middle Westerners feel they had had a share in the visit," she wrote. "After which they would rally enthusiastically behind any cause represented by the King and Queen!"[23] Halifax admitted that "there was some force in these representations", but the idea did not get anywhere, apparently due to opposition both from Roosevelt and from the Canadians, who were concerned that this extra leg would be at the expense of time spent by the royal visitors in their own country.

The same was true of a proposal by Culbert Olson, the newly elected governor of California, that the King and Queen slip across the border while they were in Vancouver to visit San Francisco, and an official request by North Dakota that a visit there should be included in the royal itinerary. "There can of course be no question of the invitation being accepted but in view of the trouble the state legislature has gone to we don't like to hurt their feelings by turning the idea down straight away," one diplomat in the British embassy wrote to the Foreign Office. "Perhaps you could in due course let us have a nicely worded reply which we could send on 'by Command of His Majesty'."[24]

There were also other details of the royal schedule to fill in. The Colonial Office suggested that while the royal couple were in New York they visit the West Indian community – an idea vetoed by Ronald Lindsay, who declared: "Not all West Indians in New York are nice. Some have tendencies which are unwisely political and almost disloyal." He was backed by the Consul General in New York who was also opposed on the grounds that "blacks [sic] are an element held in the lowest estimation, for very good reasons".[25]

There were other matters of protocol to resolve. The President was initially reluctant to accept the King's invitation to a dinner at the British embassy, since this would mean he would have to wear his leg irons two days running. He relented, but scrapped the earlier idea of accompanying his guests to New York; he would instead go directly to Hyde

Park and wait for them there. The King's wish not to address Congress was respected; the formal reason given was that it would set a precedent for addressing legislatures during subsequent state visits to other countries. It was agreed that he would instead be introduced informally to members of the Congress in the rotunda of the Capitol.

Equally ticklish was the question of which politician should accompany the King during the American part of his visit. Mackenzie King would automatically be with him during the Canadian stage, but the King thought he should be accompanied by Halifax when he crossed the forty-ninth parallel, as had been the case during his visit to Paris in July 1938. Yet taking along the British foreign secretary risked sending out the signal that the royal visit was a political one, with the aim of concluding some kind of alliance with the United States, which would have infuriated the isolationist camp. The King's next suggestion was not to take any minister along with him. This, too, was problematic, since it automatically precluded any political conversation.

For Mackenzie King, it seemed self-evident that he should accompany the King south of the border. There was still some hesitation in London, however, prompting the Canadian to express concern that "the King should cast him aside at the frontier like an old boot".[26] Mackenzie King then embarked on an extensive lobbying campaign to prevent this from happening. According to the King's official biographer, John W. Wheeler-Bennett, "He moved all heaven and earth in his determination to attend His Majesty in Washington. He harangued the Governor General; he wrote with deep feeling to the King's private secretary; he telegraphed at length to Mr Chamberlain. No stone was left unturned, no avenue unexplored."[27] That March Mackenzie King was pleased to learn his campaign had been successful. The King sent him a personal letter saying he would like him to come to the United States too.

There were also complications on the American side. As ambassador to London, Joseph Kennedy was keen to go along, not least because he was contemplating a run at the presidency in 1940; being seen alongside the President and the King would be a public-relations coup that would greatly enhance his profile. So he urged the State Department that he be allowed to play the role of guide to the royal couple.

Roosevelt was wary. The relationship between the two men dated back to 1917, when Kennedy was assistant manager of Bethlehem Steel's Fore River Shipyard in Massachusetts and Roosevelt, as assistant secretary of the Navy, was in charge of overseeing US ship production. They had clashed over two warships that the yard had built for the Argentinians and was refusing to release until they were paid for. The American government wanted them to be handed over and, to Kennedy's surprise, Roosevelt sent in the marines to seize them.

During the 1920s, Kennedy had amassed a personal fortune through dealings in the stock market, real estate,

Hollywood film production and the import of liquor from Britain and was a major backer of Roosevelt's first election campaign in 1932. When the Securities and Exchange Commission was created to clean up Wall Street in 1934, he was the surprise choice as its first president. People began to mutter about Kennedy's various financial shenanigans, but Roosevelt replied simply: "Set a thief to catch a thief."

After helping Roosevelt's successful re-election campaign in 1936, Kennedy felt he deserved a reward – and hinted that the one he had in mind was to become Secretary to the Treasury. After it was made clear to him that this was not possible, he indicated to Roosevelt's son James that he would like to be ambassador to Britain.

In his memoirs, James recalls that when he passed on the request to his father, "he laughed so hard he almost toppled from his wheelchair."[28] But the idea grew on Roosevelt: he knew the businessman in Kennedy would ensure that he negotiated hard on an Anglo-American trade agreement that was under discussion at the time and also that he was wealthy enough to entertain in grand style in London – something ambassadors were required to fund out of their own pocket. Above all, the idea of sending an Irish Catholic as Washington's representative to the Court of St James's appealed to Roosevelt's mischievous side.

Kennedy was nevertheless required to pass one bizarre test before securing the appointment: when he came to the Oval Office to press his claim to the job, Roosevelt asked him to stand by the fireplace so he could take a good look at him, and then instructed him to take down his trousers. Kennedy, though shocked, obliged. After a pause, the President told him. "Someone who saw you in a bathing suit once told me something I now know to be true. Joe, just look at your legs. You are just about the most bow-legged man I have ever seen." This mattered, Roosevelt told him, because protocol dictated that ambassadors, when presenting their credentials to the King, had to wear knee breeches and silk stockings. "When photos of our new ambassador appear all over the world, we'll be a laughing stock," he told him. "You're just not right for the job, Joe."[29]

Undaunted, Kennedy asked for two weeks to try to persuade the British to allow him to be presented at court dressed in a cutaway coat and striped trousers instead. Sure enough, he was back with an official letter within a fortnight saying the British were prepared to waive tradition on this occasion. In March 1938, accompanied by a great fanfare in the British press, he arrived in London.

Roosevelt soon came to rue his appointment. Kennedy's deep loathing of war, and of its impact both on his fortune and on his four sons, ensured that he quickly became a close friend of Chamberlain and an advocate of his policy of appeasement. He coupled this with a conviction that, if war did come, America should keep out of it. This was to put him at odds with Roosevelt, who was coming to realize the potential danger Hitler posed to the United States and appreciated the need to bolster Britain as a bulwark against Nazi expansion. As one of Roosevelt's biographers put it: "The isolationist Kennedy was ultimately widely reckoned to be, along with the Stalin-worshipping Joseph Davies in the Soviet Union, one of the worst diplomatic appointments in the history of the United States."[30]

For this reason, Roosevelt was determined that Kennedy shouldn't be involved in the trip. And so, although he had been the one who delivered the invitation to the King, it had been in a sealed envelope, and the ambassador was only aware of the contents of the letter when the King read it out to him. It was a serious embarrassment to Kennedy who, apparently at his own initiative, had mooted the idea of a royal trip to America when he and his wife, Rose, were invited for the weekend to Windsor Castle in April 1938, shortly after they arrived. The royal couple had been enthusiastic: "I only know three Americans – you, Fred Astaire and J.P. Morgan – and I would like to know more," the Queen had told him.[31]

Kennedy continued to press to be allowed to accompany the King and Queen, but was thwarted by Roosevelt. His only consolation was that he and Rose were allowed to host a dinner party for the royal couple at the ambassadorial residence in London two days before their departure in order to give them an idea of what to expect on the other side of the Atlantic. The food was Virginia ham and shad roe, both specially imported. The entertainment included a couple of Walt Disney films.

Chapter 4

Roosevelt

Thirteen years George VI's senior, Franklin D. Roosevelt, who was born on 30th January 1882 in Hyde Park, also came from a privileged background, although one that was very different from the King's. The Roosevelts were one of the oldest families in New York, of mixed English and Dutch descent, and had lived in the Hudson Valley since the nineteenth century, when FDR's great-grandfather built a house near Poughkeepsie. They had made their money from a variety of sources, including the West Indian sugar trade, shipping, real estate, coal and railway.

FDR's father, James, had inherited considerable wealth. Although involved in business ventures with varying degrees of success, he primarily lived the life of a country squire, bestriding his horse in formal English riding wear, sailing in his yacht on the Hudson in summer and in iceboats in the winter. In 1866, while married to his first wife, Rebecca Howland – a cousin, in the usual Roosevelt fashion – he bought a Colonial-style clapboard house set in 1,300 acres of woodland, with glorious views of the valley. He and his wife gradually added to the property, until it eventually grew to have thirty-five rooms and nine baths. Other wealthy families were also attracted to the area: in 1895, Frederick William Vanderbilt – whose grandfather, Cornelius Vanderbilt, had been the richest man in America in his day – built a mansion down the road.

Although the house was formally called Springwood, most people knew it simply as Hyde Park. It was there that the couple's first and only son, James Roosevelt Roosevelt, was born. This "double Roosevelt" was a way for his father to boast of his proud family name and also to avoid the "junior" form, which he disliked. The boy soon became known to friends and family as "Rosey".

Rebecca died in 1876, and after an abortive attempt to marry another cousin, James walked down the aisle again in 1880 with Sara Delano, a member of a family of French Huguenots who had come to America in the seventeenth century and had a pedigree that was even more illustrious than his.

James was already fifty-three when Franklin was born, and Sara, twenty-six years his junior, soon established herself as the dominant influence in their son's life. While most families as wealthy as the Roosevelts put their newborn babies in the care of nurses or old family retainers, Sara insisted on doing everything herself and took care of her son for almost a year, even though a wet nurse was available. She was also determined that he should grow up a Delano as much as a Roosevelt: his first name came from her favourite uncle. "My son is a Delano, not a Roosevelt at all," she once declared.

The birth was a difficult one, and Sara was advised to avoid a second and potentially fatal pregnancy. This left her free to devote her life to Franklin: he was schooled at home, initially by Sara herself, and then by a series of governesses and tutors who followed a rigorous study plan that she had drawn up. Playmates were carefully selected from the ranks of the other suitable families that lived along the Hudson. While other children were learning their ABCs in English, Franklin was doing so in French and German too, and soon became fluent in both languages. His father taught him to ride and hunt and also to sail at Campobello, a Canadian island off the coast of Maine, where the family had a summer retreat.

Franklin's life changed in 1890, when he was eight: his father suffered a mild heart attack and gradually became an invalid. The riding and sailing ended, and Sara became largely responsible for the rest of their son's upbringing. As an only child raised on a rural estate, the boy spent much of his time in the company of adults; frequent family vacations in Europe broadened his horizons and helped him develop his linguistic skills. At the age of twelve he should have gone off to prep school with his contemporaries, but Sara could not bear to part with him; it was only when he reached fourteen that he finally escaped her influence, attending Groton, a prestigious boarding school that aimed at producing young gentlemen fit to rule the nation. Even then, he still could not escape his mother: when he was quarantined in the school infirmary with scarlet fever, he was astonished to hear a tapping on his window and saw her perched on the top of a workman's ladder. She returned every day to read to him until he had recovered.[1]

Just five foot three inches and weighing barely seven stone, Franklin was a sickly child, and already suffered from the frequent colds, throat infections and bouts of sinusitis that would plague him all his life. At Harvard, he was only a C-student, but was a member of the prestigious Alpha Delta Phi fraternity and became editor-in-chief of the *Harvard Crimson* newspaper. It was while he was studying there that his fifth cousin, Theodore Roosevelt, became vice president and then, in September 1901, after the assassination of President William McKinley, moved into the White House. Although a Republican, Theodore attempted to move his party in a progressive direction and was elected president in his own right in 1904.

FDR went on to Columbia Law School and began his career as a corporate lawyer, but was keen to follow his cousin into politics – although for the Democrats. He scored his first success in 1910, running for the New York State Senate for the district of Poughkeepsie, which included Hyde Park. The area was solidly Republican, but the cachet of the family name, coupled with FDR's energy and reform-ing zeal, brought him victory, even though he was still only twenty-eight. Typically, when a friend had proposed that he stand for political office, Franklin's response had been: "Sounds like a good idea, I'll have to discuss it with Mother."

Roosevelt became an instant celebrity in Albany, the capital of New York State, with his progressive views and willingness to take on Tammany Hall, the powerful and often corrupt political machine that controlled New York Democratic politics. He also backed Woodrow Wilson's successful candidacy for the party in the 1912 presidential election; Wilson repaid Roosevelt for his support after he took office in March 1913 by naming him assistant secretary of the Navy – a post that Theodore had held for a year in the late 1890s during his own rise to the top.

Like his distant cousin before him, FDR had his sights set on higher things. In 1914, he tried to win the Democrats' backing to run for the US Senate seat for New York; although he did not succeed, he remained undaunted. He fared better in 1920, when he resigned from his Navy job and won his party's nomination for the vice presidency, on a ticket headed by Governor James M. Cox of Ohio. At thirty-eight, he was four years younger than his cousin Teddy had been when he was nominated for the same post by the Republicans.

Yet, while Teddy had been successful, Franklin's attempt ended in failure: Cox was soundly beaten by Warren G. Harding, who promised Americans a "return to normalcy" after the turmoil of the Wilson years and won sixty-one per cent of the vote – the greatest percentage achieved by a party since 1820. Roosevelt went back to New York to practise law. Observers thought his political ambitions over. They were wrong: he was playing the long game.

As he told Cox, Roosevelt realized the Democrats would not get back into power until the Republicans were driven out by an economic collapse, and he set out to reposition himself in order to benefit from that moment when it came. In the meantime, he was determined to earn some more money in order to reduce his dependence on his mother. Making full use of his political contacts, he joined the Fidelity & Deposit Company of Maryland, as vice president for New York, New Jersey and New England, earning $25,000 a year – five times more than he had made in the Navy – and having to work only half-days.

Then, in August the following year, came another event that was to change his life for ever. While vacationing at Campobello, Roosevelt contracted an illness that led to permanent paralysis from the waist down. It was diagnosed as polio, even though this has since been doubted: his age – thirty-nine – at the onset of the disease, coupled with his symptoms, has led to suggestions that it was actually Guillain–Barré syndrome, a rare disorder affecting the peripheral nervous system that leads to paralysis, starting in the feet and moving up to the trunk. Whatever the cause, Roosevelt refused to accept that he would be permanently paralysed for the rest of his life. He tried various treatments, and in 1926 bought a resort at Warm Springs, a spa in Georgia, where he founded a hydrotherapy centre for the treatment of polio patients.

Despite his defeat in 1920, Roosevelt was determined to continue his political career. He strongly believed that in order to do so he would have to convince people he was getting better. And so began what was to be an extraordinary exercise in deception. Although he used a wheelchair in private, he was careful not to be seen in it in public. In March 1922, after seven months in which he only lay or sat, he was fitted by doctors with a pair of leg irons weighing a stone: stretching from his heels to above his waist, and secured with a leather pelvic band, they allowed him to stand up, if precariously, as if on stilts. He then developed a method of walking a short distance by swivelling his torso while supporting himself with crutches or a cane. "It was inelegant, hazardous and exhausting, but it was progress and a great refreshment to Roosevelt's morale," wrote one biographer.[2]

Even after he became president, Roosevelt was to make great efforts to ensure he was not shown in the press in a way that would reveal his disability. In public, he would usually appear standing upright, leaning on one side or on an aide or one of his sons. Only two photographs are known to have been taken of him in his wheelchair; only a few seconds of footage exist of the special walk he perfected.

By the late 1920s, Roosevelt was ready to revive his political ambitions. In 1928, when his mentor, Alfred E. Smith, stepped down from the governorship of New York to make an unsuccessful bid for the presidency, Roosevelt secured the Democratic nomination and was elected by a narrow one-per-cent margin. As a reformist governor, he instituted a number of social programmes; when he was re-elected two years later, the margin had grown to fourteen per cent.

As governor of the country's most populous state, Roosevelt was the Democratic Party's obvious candidate for the 1932 presidential election, even though this meant pushing past Smith. In his speech accepting the nomination, he promised a "new deal for the American people", adding: "This is more than a political campaign. It is a call to arms."

The poll was held in the midst of the Great Depression; the promises of Herbert Hoover, the Republican incumbent, to bring about a new era of prosperity had ended in plunging industrial production and incomes and huge rises in the number of homeless and the unemployment rate, which was to peak at twenty-five per cent. Hoover stood little chance. With the Democratic Party united behind him and a leading southern conservative, John Nance Garner, the speaker of the House of Representatives, as his running mate, Roosevelt achieved a landslide victory, winning 57.4 per cent of the popular vote and taking forty-two states to just six for Hoover. The election marked a turning point in American political history: Roosevelt managed to assemble a new majority coalition for the Democrats made up of organized labour, African Americans, Jews and Italian and

Polish Americans that was to dominate most presidential elections for the three decades that followed.

Roosevelt's inauguration on 4th March 1933 coincided with another twist in the country's economic woes: a bank crisis, prompting him to utter his famous phrase: "The only thing we have to fear is fear itself." The next day, Congress passed an Emergency Banking Act, which defused the crisis. It was one among a record number of bills and executive orders during the first hundred days of Roosevelt's presidency. These formed the first stage of what became known, after his 1932 convention speech, as the "New Deal", the focus of which was on providing "relief, recovery and reform". Such measures began to bring benefits, but the economy was still in a parlous state when Roosevelt stood for a second term in 1936. Standing against Alf Landon, the governor of Kansas, who fought a lacklustre campaign, his victory was even greater: he increased his share of the popular vote to 60.8 per cent, carrying all but two states.

FDR's private life was more complex – and understandable only in terms of the dominant role played by his mother Sara, which was to continue until her death in 1941, two weeks before her eighty-seventh birthday. This made it all the more surprising that when he came to marry, he chose a woman of whom his mother disapproved.

Anna Eleanor Roosevelt was the daughter of Elliott Roosevelt, the younger brother of Theodore, the future president, and Anna Hall Roosevelt. Two years younger than

Franklin and a distant cousin, she was born at 56 West 37th Street in New York City, into a world of immense wealth and privilege. Nicknamed "Granny" by her family, she had an old-fashioned manner. At a time when a great premium was put on physical beauty, she was not a pretty child – a fact that, cruelly, was often pointed out to her. "Eleanor, I hardly know what's to happen to you. You're so plain that you really have nothing to do except be good," her mother once said to her as she was playing with a cousin.[3] Other comments followed, both to her face and behind her back, leaving an enduring mark. "I often felt that I'd like to have the floor open so that I could sink into it," she once said.[4]

Eleanor's life took a tragic turn: when she was eight, her mother died of diphtheria; a year later, the same disease claimed her four-year-old brother, Elliott Jr. To add to her woes, her father was an alcoholic. After a series of failed cures and stays in sanatoriums, he collapsed and died at the age of thirty-four. Already before his death, Eleanor and her surviving younger brother, Hall, had been sent to live with their maternal grandmother, Mary Ludlow Hall, who had a home in New York City and an estate at Tivoli on the Hudson. It was a depressing life, and Eleanor felt lonely, unloved and insecure. Although growing tall and with wavy, honey-coloured hair and a flawless complexion, she seemed reconciled to not being a great beauty. "It may seem strange but no matter how plain a woman may be, if truth and loyalty are stamped upon her face all will be attracted to her and she will do good to all who come near her and those who know her well will always love her," she wrote optimistically when aged fifteen.[5]

Escape came later that year when the family sent her to Allenswood Academy, a small finishing school for the daughters of wealthy Americans and Europeans near Wimbledon on the south-west outskirts of London. The headmistress, Marie Souvestre, was a French feminist who, at a time when little attention was paid to the education of women, taught her girls to think critically. Eleanor grew much more confident and self-assured during her stay, despite the school's curious rules, one of which was a requirement that, after lunch, the girls lie on the floor for an hour and a half and fix their minds on a single thought that would then be discussed at teatime.

Eleanor would have liked to stay on when her three years were up, but in the summer of 1902, at the age of seventeen, she was ordered back to America by her grandmother to be formally presented to New York society. It was shortly after her return that, while travelling on a train from New York to Poughkeepsie, she happened across Franklin. As distant cousins, they already knew each other vaguely from previous encounters and soon fell into conversation; Franklin even took her to the Pullman car in which his mother was sitting. They met again by chance a few weeks later, when they found themselves in the same private box at the National Horse Show at Madison Square Garden; then, that New

Year's Eve, along with other members of the Roosevelt clan, they were both at a reception in the White House following Theodore's election as president in his own right.

It was during the course of 1903 that their relationship appears to have begun in earnest. It was a curious match: still somewhat old-maidish in appearance, Eleanor had little in common with the glamorous society girls usually frequented by Franklin, who had become a tall, handsome and physically vital young man. Yet she offered him the kind of intellectual companionship that he had hitherto found only among his fellow male students at Harvard. She also encouraged him to take an interest in social issues, bringing him along on tours of the East Side slums of New York, where she taught the underprivileged. To the ambitious Franklin, there was the lure of social advancement too: the Oyster Bay branch of the Roosevelt family, to which Eleanor belonged, was much more prestigious than Franklin's Hyde Park one – not least because it counted Theodore among its members.

It was only that November, when the Delano family was gathered at the family seat in Fairhaven, Massachusetts, for their annual Thanksgiving get-together, that Franklin broke the news to his mother: a few days earlier he had proposed to Eleanor. It was like a bombshell. Although Sara had met Eleanor several times since their first encounter on the train and had even welcomed her to the family retreat on Campobello Island, it had never occurred to her that there was any romantic attachment between her and Franklin. It was not just the shock felt by a possessive mother of losing her only son to another woman. Sara was convinced her son could do better for himself than Eleanor. And so, although unable to prevent the match – her son was twenty-one, after all – she did the next best thing: she begged him not to say anything and give it a year. "Franklin gave me quite a startling announcement," she wrote that evening in her diary.[6]

Sara continued to hope that her son would change his mind. That winter she took him off on a six-week Caribbean cruise with a Harvard room-mate; maybe distance would take his mind off his still secret fiancée. Her efforts were to no avail. Franklin and Eleanor's engagement was announced on 1st December 1904; they married on 17th March the following year, St Patrick's Day. The day was chosen so that Theodore Roosevelt, in New York for the parade, could give her away – squeezing in the duty between the parade itself and two speeches. "Well, Franklin, there's nothing like keeping the name in the family," Theodore told him after they had exchanged their vows.

Although she had little alternative but to accept Eleanor, Sara retained her grip on her son. Before the marriage, she had embarked on a mission of shaping her future daughter-in-law. This continued after the couple returned from their honeymoon, a three-month trip through Britain, France and Italy. Sara had leased for them a four-storey brownstone at 125 East 36th Street in New York, a mere three blocks from her own home in the city. She had furnished it herself and hired the servants.

Eleanor, still only twenty when she married and without a mother of her own, was in many ways grateful for her mother-in-law's advice. She was also stifled by it, and the two women began to clash over the rearing of the children, the first of whom, Anna, was born in May 1906, followed by James a year and a half later. Sara was soon to step up her influence even further: at Christmas 1907 she announced she was giving the couple as a present a new five-storey brownstone. The house, at 47 East 65th Street, completed the following year, just happened to adjoin a similar property she was building for herself. The house's conception, design and interior decoration were completely in the hands of Franklin and his mother. Eleanor was not even allowed onto the premises until the house was finished.

Living next door meant Sara was now able to intervene in every aspect of her son and daughter-in-law's lives. The two houses were linked by doors at every level, allowing her to check up on dinner-party arrangements and make sure her growing brood of grandchildren was being looked after properly. The Roosevelts' fourth child, Elliott, born in September 1910, recalled how, when his mother was entertaining guests to tea, his grandmother would often arrive and, unbidden, take over the role of hostess. "This was a constant, nagging problem for mother in her own development of her own household abilities from the earliest years," he said.[7] It was little better in summer when the whole family would decamp to Campobello Island, where they vacationed in adjoining homes.

Eleanor was to gain a measure of independence from her mother-in-law when Franklin was elected to the New York State Senate that November and they moved to Albany. She gained even more with the move to Washington that came with her husband's appointment as assistant secretary to the Navy. This time they lived in a house found not by Sara but by Eleanor's aunt Anna, known in the family as Bye.

While Sara's sway over Franklin and Eleanor was waning, another woman, whose influence was to be even more disruptive, was looming on the horizon. Overwhelmed by the demands of Washington society and pregnant for a fifth time, Eleanor decided she needed help. Aunt Bye had a solution in the form of Lucy Mercer, the eighteen-year-old daughter of a suitably well-connected family that had fallen on hard times. After a brief interview, Eleanor took her on to work three mornings at a salary of $30 a week.

Personable and efficient, Lucy dealt with all the invitations, bills and other paperwork, and got on well with the Roosevelt children. She was also very attractive: at five foot nine, she was slightly shorter than Eleanor, and had blue eyes, a milky complexion, light-brown hair and a regal posture. In character, the two women were very different: Eleanor was earnest and oblivious to fashion, and had, according to Elliott, "something of a schoolmarm's air about her". Lucy, by contrast, was poised, glamorous and self-assured. As one of her cousins put it: "Every man who ever knew her fell in love with her."

Roosevelt was soon among them. It is not certain when his relationship with Lucy began, though it is thought to have been some time in 1916. It is very clear when it came to light, however. In September 1918, he returned from a two-month inspection trip to the Front in Europe so badly ill with influenza that when the *Leviathan*, the warship on which he was travelling, docked in New York, he was met by a doctor and an ambulance. Since his own home was by then let out, he was taken, much to Sara's satisfaction, to her house. While he was in bed, Eleanor, distraught, started to unpack his bags. Concern for her husband's health was soon to turn into an overwhelming sense of betrayal: tucked away amid the clothes and toiletries, she came across a bundle of lightly scented letters that revealed he was having an affair with Lucy.

The extent of their relationship and whether it extended to sex is not clear; it would certainly have been difficult for them to have conducted a full-blown clandestine affair. Franklin's house was full of servants, and Lucy still lived with her mother. A tryst in a Washington hotel, where FDR was already well known, would have been tricky. Plus, Lucy was a devout Catholic who regarded sex with a married man as a cardinal sin. The incriminating letters, presumably destroyed, have never been seen by historians. Whatever the truth, Eleanor was devastated: the man whom she had loved and supported and by whom she had had six children had betrayed her with another woman who was younger, livelier and more attractive than her – and worse, was her own social secretary. Twenty-five years later she wrote: "The bottom dropped out of my own particular world and I faced myself, my surroundings, my world, honestly for the first time."[8]

Although concerned about the prospect of her children growing up without a father, Eleanor did not want to remain trapped in a loveless marriage, and offered her husband a divorce. Franklin, completely besotted with Lucy, appears seriously to have considered the possibility, even though it would have certainly provoked a family crisis. At this point Sara, who was still paying Franklin's household expenses despite his $5,000-a-year naval job and Eleanor's own income from her family, intervened. She told her son that if he left his wife she would "not give him another dollar". Nor would she allow him to inherit his beloved Springwood. Roosevelt was also warned by Louis Howe, a former newspaperman turned trusted political adviser, that a divorce would mean the end of his chances of winning elective office.

Faced with the loss of family, money, his ancestral home and his political career, Roosevelt agreed to remain married. But Eleanor would allow him to do so only under two conditions: he had to break off with Mercer immediately and could never again share his wife's bed – something that appears to have caused little concern to Eleanor herself, who once told her daughter she considered sex an ordeal that women must bear. Roosevelt agreed to the conditions. As their son, James, wrote later, "After that father and mother had an armed truce that endured to the day he died, despite several occasions I was to observe in which he, in one way or another, held out his arms to mother and she flatly refused to enter his embrace."[9] Lucy fled to her relatives, and in February 1920 married Winthrop Rutherfurd, a wealthy widower twenty-nine years her senior. As Joseph E. Persico, who has charted the affair in his book, *Franklin and Lucy*, put it: "In the end, the three parties in the triangle behaved according to character, Eleanor self-sacrificing, Franklin self-preserving, Lucy lovelorn but resilient."[10]

Roosevelt's illness was to bring him and Eleanor closer again, if only temporarily: she nursed him during the first agonizing weeks, but soon found it a challenge to care for him, and Roosevelt began to tire of her exhortations to do exercises. In the spring of 1922, he left the bustle of their New York apartment and retreated to Springwood, which was largely empty.

Their marriage had already changed from a conventional union into something more akin to a political partnership – and one in which Eleanor found herself in a more powerful position. Indeed, the events of 1918 ultimately proved to have been something of a liberation for her. She had spent the first dozen years of marriage entirely in her husband's shadow, whether helping him fulfil his ambitions or bearing him six children – all the while overseen by Sara. Now she felt free to go her own way, entering a community of politically aware women who shared her passion for social reform. While her husband was pursuing his political career, she began to make a name for herself in her own right, organizing conferences, serving on committees and helping raise funds for the Democratic Party.

Eleanor was also developing a network of independent-minded women friends – among them prominent lesbian couples such as Elizabeth Read and Esther Lape, and Nan Cook and Marion Dickerman. Such friendships inevitably led to gossip, fuelled by her acerbic cousin Alice Roosevelt Longworth. Never too fond of Eleanor, she was heard remarking loudly in a fashionable Washington restaurant, "I don't care what they say, I simply cannot believe that Eleanor Roosevelt is a lesbian."[11]

During the 1920s Eleanor regularly visited the home in Greenwich Village that Read, an attorney and scholar of international affairs, shared with Lape, a college professor, having dinner, reading poetry and discussing progressive ideas. Her involvement with Cook and Dickerman became even closer: in 1924, they built a fieldstone cottage named Val-Kill, with a swimming pool next to it, on a piece of land donated by Roosevelt in the grounds of the Hyde Park estate. Dubbed by FDR "the love nest" and "Honeymoon

Cottage", it rapidly turned into the three women's private domain. Other joint projects followed: in 1925, they founded a newsletter, *Women's Democratic News*, and the following year they bought the Todhunter School for Girls in New York City, where Dickerman became principal and Eleanor a teacher. Then, in 1927, they opened a factory at Val-Kill in which they made handcrafted reproductions of early American furniture: Cook became manager and Eleanor its sales agent.

Such friendships, as Rodger Strcitmatter, an expert on the First Lady, put it, "show that love between women was definitely not an alien concept for Eleanor. She was a professed believer in sexual freedom – including people acting on homosexual desires. In 1925, she wrote in her personal journal: 'No form of love is to be despised.'"[12]

The real love of Eleanor's life, however, was a pioneering woman journalist named Lorena Hickok – or "Hick", as everyone called her. Weighing in at fourteen stone and often with a whiskey glass in her hand and cigar in her mouth, Hick was an extraordinary character who rose from humble origins to become one of America's leading reporters and the first woman to have her byline on the front page of the *New York Times*. She was also a lesbian, living for eight years from 1918 with Ellie Morse, whom she encountered when they were both working at the *Minneapolis Tribune*.

Hick met Eleanor in 1928 while covering politics for the Associated Press, America's biggest news network, out of

75

its New York office. In that year's presidential election, she focused on the campaigns of the New York governor, Alfred E. Smith – who was to be soundly beaten by Herbert Hoover – and of Roosevelt.

It was far from love at first sight: Eleanor, Hick wrote later, "was very plain". Yet the future First Lady was also an intelligent and forceful woman whose many activities in the social sphere made her newsworthy. Reluctant to be pigeonholed as someone who wrote about "women's issues", Hick avoided covering Eleanor. That changed in 1932, when Roosevelt stood for the presidency and Hick was sent to cover his campaign. This meant talking to the candidate's wife, who had become one of his most trusted advisers. Hick returned from her first interview with Eleanor smitten. The feeling was mutual: time and time again, Eleanor would pluck Hick out from among the gaggle of reporters whenever they met on the campaign trail. They became even closer in October that year, when another female reporter who had been covering Eleanor moved to San Francisco and Hick, as the only woman left in the bureau, was given the job.

Infatuated, Hick painted an increasingly flattering picture of the would-be First Lady in her articles, some of which, in a clear breach of usual journalistic rules, she handed over to be vetted by the Roosevelt campaign before sending them to her editors. Objectivity went out of the window: it became her aim to ensure that the Roosevelts made it into the White House.

Shortly after FDR's victory, Hick bowed to the inevitable: in June 1933 she left journalism and, with Eleanor's help, secured a job as chief investigator for the Federal Emergency Relief Administration, crossing America to report on the effectiveness of the various programmes that had been introduced. She also gave public-relations advice to the First Lady, encouraging her to carve out a profile independent of her husband's. At Hick's suggestion, Eleanor began to hold weekly press conferences and, starting in 1935, wrote a syndicated column entitled 'My Day' – which, over the years that followed, was to provide an extraordinary fly-on-the-wall insight into the life of the first couple.

The true nature of the relationship between the two women was long a matter of debate – were they merely friends or actually lovers? Any such ambiguity seemed to be dispelled in 1978, when the Franklin D. Roosevelt Library opened eighteen cardboard boxes containing 3,500 letters that the women wrote to each other during their thirty-year friendship. They included passages that were gushingly affectionate and sometimes even openly erotic. "I wish I could lie down beside you and take you in my arms," Eleanor wrote to her friend, whom she addressed as "Hick Dearest". Hick, away on work in Minnesota, wrote on 5th December 1933: "I've been trying today to bring back your face – to remember just how you look [...]. Most clearly, I remember your eyes, with a kind of teasing smile in them, and the feeling of that soft spot just north-east of the corner of your mouth against my lips."[13]

Yet some experts on Eleanor have been appalled at the suggestion she was a lesbian. They noted that she often wrote in a florid style, even to her mother-in-law, with whom her relations were cool. Arthur Schlesinger Jr said it was important "not to read twentieth-century preoccupations into nineteenth-century forms of personal relationships". Franklin D. Roosevelt Jr, the literary executor of his mother's estate, also warned against attaching too much significance to Eleanor's prose style. "Remember, my mother was brought up in an era when children read the Brontës and Jane Austen, and they adopted that effusive form of writing," he said.[14]

Chapter 5

Daisy

It was shortly afterwards that another woman, Margaret Suckley, entered Roosevelt's life. Born on 20th December 1891, she was the fifth child and first daughter of Robert Brown Suckley (pronounced "Sookley"), the son of a Hudson River gentleman, and Elizabeth Montgomery, the daughter of an Episcopal clergyman. She was known in the family as Daisy, from the French word for that flower, *marguerite*.

Robert Suckley had a New York law practice, but, as Daisy later put it, "he never worried much about it".[1] At the age of thirty-two, he had inherited his father's considerable real-estate fortune and preferred to spend summers abroad and winters on an iceboat on the Hudson. They lived at Rhinebeck, in New York State. Their family home, Wilderstein, had been a fairly simple two-storey Italianate villa when he inherited it from his father in 1888. He felt it was not grand enough to bring up his own family in, though, and employed Arnout Cannon, a Poughkeepsie architect, to transform it into an extraordinary turreted, five-storey Queen Anne mansion with thirty-five rooms.

The Suckleys' fortune took a turn for the worse following the collapse of the property market in 1893 and the failure of some other investments four years later. The family simply shut up the house, which required a staff of nearly twenty to run, and decamped to Château-d'Oex, in Switzerland, where they spent ten years. It was an unusual existence: they lived at the Hôtel Rosa, and Daisy and her three brothers and two sisters were taught by a Mademoiselle Blum, who would rap their knuckles with a ruler if they failed to remember their lessons. There were few other children in the hotel, which meant they lacked playmates. Instead, the Alps became their playground: in summer they would go on family outings walking in the mountains; in the winter, they would do cross-country skiing.

They returned to Wilderstein when Daisy was fifteen. Her father wanted her to go to college, but her mother was opposed on the grounds that it made girls "unworldly" and, worse, unmarriageable. Daisy, who was to gain considerable experience in maintaining the peace within her turbulent family, proposed a compromise: she would go to Bryn Mawr in Pennsylvania, but for just two years and then return home to help her mother care for the family.

Attractive, bright, witty and well read, Daisy always looked and acted much older than she really was and would dress according to the fashions of her parents' generation. This did not prevent several men from courting her, but Daisy did not come close to marrying any of them. She seemed, according to one relative, "adamantly uninterested in sex" – a reflection of the attitude of her mother, who considered it such an ordeal that she invariably wept at weddings at the thought of what horrors lay in store for the bride.[2]

The First World War broadened Daisy's horizons: during the summer she sold war bonds door to door in Rhinebeck and in winter she worked as a nurse's aide on Ellis Island. It also marked the final decline of the Suckleys: in 1917, her eldest brother, Henry, on whom the family's hopes had been pinned, was killed in Salonika, Greece, when the Red Cross ambulance he was driving was hit by a German bomb. Then, four years later, her father, whom she had worshipped and whose side she had taken in his frequent arguments with her mother, died of a heart attack, aged sixty-five.

From then on, Daisy resolved to look after her mother and her surviving brothers, Robert and Arthur. She had her work cut out. Although both attended Harvard, neither graduated or held down jobs, and they both continued to live at Wilderstein. To add to the family's woes, Robert, who had been left in charge of most of what remained of the family fortune, in the early 1920s invested much of it in German marks, which were rendered worthless by hyperinflation. All but a little of the rest went in the Wall Street Crash of 1929. In order to keep the house going, Daisy took a job as paid companion to her elderly invalid aunt, Sophie, who was Mrs Woodbury G. Langdon. This meant spending part of her time at Langdon's apartment on Park Avenue in New

York and the rest at Mansakenning, her summer house just down the road from Wilderstein. By the early 1930s, the Suckley family's fortune was close to its nadir: they no longer had any servants, had been forced to sell their home in Manhattan and were largely dependent on the salary Daisy was paid by her aunt.

It was in 1910 that Daisy had first met Roosevelt, a sixth cousin once removed, through William Beekman, a member of another influential family. It was at a New Year's party, one of the few such events Daisy attended, at Crumwold, a huge chateau owned by Archibald Rogers, down the river from Wilderstein. Daisy was just eighteen; Roosevelt was twenty-eight, and already married to Eleanor, but, as Daisy later told a friend, she never forgot the sight of him whirling partner after partner around the dance floor. She would go on to see him from time to time when he visited Hyde Park while pursuing his political career in Washington.

Then, in the spring of 1922, Daisy received a call from Sara Roosevelt, asking her to come to tea at Springwood. Sara explained her son's affliction and said he was lonely and needed company. The call may have seemed a curious one for a woman always conscious of the need to maintain the appearance of propriety, but Daisy was somehow acceptable, either because she was dowdy and retiring or, maybe, because she was a relative, albeit a distant one – not that this would have been considered a deterrent among the Roosevelts with their predilection for intermarriage.

That spring and summer, for several afternoons a week, Daisy would sit quietly on the lawn at Hyde Park as Roosevelt dragged himself around a set of exercise bars, keeping her entertained by telling her extravagant stories. "I'm not going to be conquered by a childish disease," he told her time and again. Daisy, in turn, was impressed by his determination. "My God, he was brave," she remembered later.[3] They continued to see each other through the 1920s. In 1928, when Roosevelt returned to politics and ran for governor of New York, Daisy began to put together a collection of newspaper clippings charting his daily activities.

It was after Roosevelt became president and invited Daisy to his inauguration in 1933 that their friendship really began in earnest. "A Red Letter Day: The President of the United States of America rang me up on the telephone!" she wrote in her diary on 1st August.[4] Then, three days later, Eleanor called to invite Daisy and her aunt to tea at Springwood. It was while they were there that Roosevelt made a suggestion that clearly thrilled Daisy. "Asked me to drive alone with him on Monday aft," she wrote. "I haven't told the family yet!!!…"

Sadly, Daisy's account of what happened that Monday is all too brief. "The Pres. & I drive in his roadster through his woods – followed by 4 detectives in a state trooper car," she wrote. "On our return Pres. shows me more books; also illustrations of birds, etc. Mrs [Eleanor] R. somewhat surprised to see me!"

More rides in the blue Ford roadster followed, interspersed with chatty letters. In a diary entry dated 9th September 1935, Daisy recalled a drive in pouring rain with the President, during which they took shelter beneath the trees on Dutchess Hill, a secluded hilltop on the Roosevelt property. From then on the pair would refer to the forested ridge as "our hill".

Another, on 22nd September, along the winding back roads through the beautiful Hudson River country in which they parked in the same place, appeared to have a special significance. "Something happened in that place on that afternoon that neither of them ever forgot," wrote Geoffrey C. Ward in his commentary on Daisy's diary. "Three years later, FDR was still calling it the beginning of a 'voyage'. Perhaps they simply kissed." A poem, entitled 'Eros', which Daisy clipped and pasted carefully into her diary for that day, suggested that they did. Or perhaps, Ward continued, "they merely confessed to each other the loneliness they felt. Certainly they talked of a special bond of friendship and agreed to share some of their secret thoughts, by letter and long-distance telephone and in person whenever they could arrange to be together."[5]

Whatever happened, Roosevelt rather impetuously suggested to Daisy that she accompany him that very night on a train journey across the country to inaugurate the Boulder Dam and then on a fishing voyage off Baja California. Eleanor was due to go as far as the Pacific but not to join

84

him on the ship. Daisy declined – either out of a sense of propriety or because of her commitment to her aunt. Yet she was clearly tempted. In a long letter to Roosevelt that she started almost the moment his train had left, she wrote: "Do you realize the amount of willpower that was necessary to refuse a certain invitation this past week? A slightly righteous feeling, I find, gives no satisfaction whatsoever – only irritation."[6] Daisy wrote many more pages to him in the weeks he was away in a friendly and increasingly intimate tone, which the President reciprocated.

After Roosevelt's return, there followed many more drives that autumn. Daisy was also finding herself drawn into one of his pet projects: building a cottage for himself on the Hyde Park estate, which he described later as "a small place to go to escape the mob", and a haven to which he planned ultimately to retire with a favourite lady to write his memoirs and detective stories.

The location was obvious: "our hill". The first step, as the President noted in a letter to Daisy in February 1936, was to build an all-weather road through the woods to the site. "I need a young woman – resident of Dutchess Co. – experienced in gardening and trees & hilltops to help me to try it out," he wrote to her on 24th February. "Perhaps by then one will apply for the job – There are other qualifications I have in mind – so difficult – yet I hope, really believe, just the right kind of applicant will turn up. Luckily I am to be the sole judge."[7]

On 7th March came Daisy's flirtatious response: "As to the 'young woman' specialist you require for laying out your Hill road, I know just the person – only she's not so young, and she won't be available until after May 15th [when Mrs Langdon planned to move back to Rhinebeck]. Perhaps the best thing would be for you to lay out the road, earlier, and then get her to approve – It won't be difficult I'm sure. And I'm quite sure she'd love the job."[8]

Pasted to the letter was a newspaper clipping from Massachusetts reporting that the local police were clamping down on "one-arm driving". "Police Chief Frank T. Coughlin does not tend to interfere with Cupid but he insisted today one-arm driving must cease," said the article. "Swains can park and spark right on Main Street, he said, and police will not bother them. But when the cars are in motion both hands must be on the wheel." Daisy had underlined the last seven words in pen. "This clipping will make you realize that people really are trying to prevent motor accidents!" she wrote. "I'm sure you approve of such a ruling and that it should be strictly enforced."[9]

And so it went on. Such flirtatious comments were typical of the correspondence between them. Quite how far their relationship went remains unclear, though Daisy certainly felt nervous about what other people thought. Writing to Roosevelt after a lunch, she said how helpful it had been that his family had been there as well. "It is so much better so, & does not raise so many eyebrows!" she wrote on 21st

September 1937.[10] On another occasion, she complained about his sending letters by special delivery, which made Aunt Sophie aware of the identity of the sender.

Such was the importance of the cottage to both Roosevelt and Suckley that in the late summer of 1937 they began drawing up their first sketches of it – and of imagining their future life there together. "Part of the time – whether or not induced by the open fire, I don't know – I was some 12 miles from here, on a Hill, sitting before a fire also – very near the corner of the sofa," Daisy wrote. "Someone was reading aloud – two french windows on each side of the fireplace, opened onto a porch – Outside – it was dark under the trees & a wind rustled what remained of autumn leaves – Across the length of the back of the room were bookshelves right up to the ceiling – In the middle, a door opening onto a terrace facing East!" A few days later, on a piece of paper with sketches of the house, she wrote: "I have made a quite perfect floor plan – but suddenly realize that the chimney will stick up in a very queer place."[11]

In early 1938, Roosevelt sent sketches to Henry J. Toombs, an architect friend who had designed various projects for him, among them Eleanor's Val-Kill. The plan, as the President envisaged it, was for a cottage in three sections: in the centre was a large living room with an open porch facing westwards towards the Hudson and the Catskills. Two symmetrical wings on either side contained bedrooms, a kitchen and a pantry. It was designed for ease of access for someone in a wheelchair: a ramp ran up to one side of the porch, and inside the floor was completely flat, with no thresholds between rooms. The windows were low. Though described as a cottage, it was actually quite substantial, with some 4,515 square feet of floor space including the porch.

The cottage quickly became a subject of public discussion – not all of it positive. Toombs listed the President as the architect, with himself merely as associate – provoking a stinging rebuke from John Lloyd Wright, the son of the celebrated architect. "The moral breakdown of the integrity and dignity of the architectural profession seems now complete," Lloyd Wright wrote to *Life* magazine. An architect from Middletown, New Jersey, noted sarcastically that he awaited "pictures of 'Doctor' Roosevelt performing an appendectomy".[12] Others joined in, pointing out faults in the design. Why did a bathroom window open onto the entrance terrace, one commentator wanted to know. Another questioned the lack of suitable wardrobe space in the bedrooms.

Roosevelt's main preoccupation was the price. He found the original estimate, at $20,796, far too high, but thanks to twenty-four cost-cutting changes, including replacing the slates on the roof with asphalt shingle and leaving the inside walls as bare plaster, he managed to reduce the bill by almost $4,500. At the time a typical local home could be bought for $1,000. "I simply cannot possibly afford to build an $18,000 house," he protested. He was also irked by

descriptions by newspapers of the cottage as "the realization of a dream" or a "dream house". It was merely "the
Roosevelt Cottage on Dutchess Hill", he insisted.[13]

Work was completed in spring 1939, but the cottage was
still almost bare. "There are now three pieces of furniture in
it," Roosevelt told the press on 30th May. "Probably by this
time next year there will be about eight. It will probably get
furnished over – I do not know what – ten or twelve years."[14]

Daisy was not the only one who dreamt of living with
Roosevelt in the cottage. The President remained fascinated
by – and an object of fascination to – several women, even
if, as Persico put it, "questions may be raised about FDR's
sexual capacity from a wheelchair".[15]

One of the principal women – and the most obvious rival
to Daisy – was Marguerite "Missy" LeHand, who had been
part of Roosevelt's life for almost two decades. Born in
September 1898 in a working-class district of Boston into
an Irish-immigrant family, she had gone straight from high
school to office work, arriving in Washington shortly before
the outbreak of war. During Roosevelt's abortive run at the
vice presidency in 1920 she joined his campaign and, though
still only twenty-two, quickly proved a key member of the
team, dealing with correspondence and helping juggle his
packed schedule. Although not a beauty in the same league
as Lucy Mercer, LeHand was always impeccably turned out
and, with her blue eyes, strong features and dark-brown, if

prematurely grey, hair pulled into a bun, she made a striking impression on all who met her.

LeHand's job came to an end with the defeat of the Democratic Party ticket, but Roosevelt took her on temporarily to help clear up the backlog of work. She did this so well that he asked her to stay on full-time. Despite the gulf between her and Roosevelt's respective backgrounds, the two soon hit it off. As Persico wrote, "LeHand matched Franklin's style, combining competence with breezy good humour. She struck a balance of self-worth while knowing her station." For her part, Daisy was amazed that "someone with 'no background at all' could possess such poise, good manners, and the appearance of breeding".[16] LeHand also endeared herself to the Roosevelt children, who had trouble pronouncing her first name: thanks to them, she became known thereafter as "Missy".

LeHand was to remain at Roosevelt's side for two decades; she had a room at Springwood and at his house in Manhattan, lived in a private apartment in the White House and accompanied him on many trips to Florida and to Warm Springs. After he became president, she proved the perfect gatekeeper, sorting out his schedule and dealing with problems that crossed his path. In the evening, after dinner, they would continue to work together in his study.

As with the other women in Roosevelt's life, the nature of his relationship with LeHand remains a matter of dispute. Some historians insist it was never consummated, a suggestion apparently supported by the way Eleanor accepted her presence and even invited her to go horse-riding with her. Others are not so sure. Either way, Elliott Roosevelt claimed his mother resented the fact that she seemed to see less of her husband than Missy, noting a comment she made years later: "Missy was young and pretty and loved a good time, and occasionally her social contacts got mixed with her work and made it hard for her and others."[17]

There were other women, too, among them Dorothy Schiff, a rich Jewish supporter of the New Deal, who in 1939 was to buy control of the *New York Post*. Slim, chic and glamorous, she made an immediate impression on Roosevelt when introduced to him in 1936, and was thereafter frequently invited to Hyde Park, where she would stay at the Val-Kill house. More than two decades younger than the President, she, like Daisy and the others, was invited to join him on hair-raising drives through the country in his Ford. "Whenever I would be slid across the front seat away from him, a strong right arm would pull me back," she recalled.[18]

Schiff's husband, George Backer, a liberal writer and Democrat activist, did not appear to mind. Much as members of the British aristocracy tolerated – or were even flattered by – their wives' liaisons with Edward VII and VIII when they were philandering Princes of Wales, so Backer, as Schiff put it, "saw it in a sort of *droit de seigneur* way, his wife being tapped by the lord of the manor".[19]

A controversial biography of Schiff, which was published in 1976, when she was seventy-three, claimed she and Roosevelt had an affair, based on interviews with her in which she made frequent use of words such as "sex object" and "turn-on" and described an occasion on which the President escorted her into the bedroom of his retreat in Hyde Park. Schiff denied the assertion, claiming subsequently: "I want to make it very clear that President Roosevelt never made a suggestion that I become his girlfriend, and Mrs Eleanor Roosevelt was just as good a friend as Mr Roosevelt."[20]

And then there was Crown Princess Märtha of Norway, who went with her children into exile in America when her country was occupied in 1940, while her husband, Crown Prince Olav, and his father, King Haakon VII, led resistance from Britain. Feminine, statuesque and looking every bit a princess, Märtha would join the President for cocktails and also go on long drives with him.

Nor did Roosevelt's break-up with Lucy Mercer – or Rutherfurd, as she had become – prove as complete as he had promised Eleanor it would be. "Given distance and long separations, the signal might become faint at times but never ceased entirely," claims Persico. "During the first hectic months of his presidency, when it seemed FDR would have time for nothing but matters of state, he made time for her."[21] She was rumoured to have attended his inauguration, hidden in the back of a limousine he sent for her. During his first hundred days in office, he received half a dozen phone calls in the White House from a Mrs Paul Johnson, who, it was subsequently revealed by Secret Service agents, was Lucy. In Roosevelt's late years, he and Lucy would begin to see each other again, and their meetings grew more frequent after her husband died in 1944.

In short, Roosevelt's personal relationships were complicated, to say the least. The contrast could not have been greater with the settled and loving family life of the man he was about to welcome to Washington and Hyde Park.

Chapter 6

Across the Atlantic

Thousands of people lined the shores of the Solent in Portsmouth as King George VI and Queen Elizabeth stepped on board the *Empress of Australia* at 2.30 p.m. on 6th May 1939, for the journey of more than three thousand miles across the Atlantic to Quebec. The royal couple had brought their two daughters, Elizabeth and Margaret Rose, on board to show them their quarters. Then they and other members of the royal family who had come to see them off posed for a photograph outside the purser's office.

The royal couple had originally planned to travel on *Repulse*, a battlecruiser which had spent almost six months from November 1938 being refitted for its special role. But as the day of their departure neared, there were misgivings about taking one of the Navy's most powerful men-of-war so far from home waters. One suggestion by the Foreign Office was that the *Repulse* take the King and Queen to America but then return immediately, leaving them to come back on a US warship. This would also have the advantage of showing the world – and Hitler and Mussolini in particular – the strength of relations between Britain and America.

Meanwhile, there were suggestions in the American press that the tense international situation meant the trip would simply have to be cancelled.

The British government was determined that the visit should go ahead, although with just eight days to go there was a change of plan: it was decided they would travel instead on the *Empress of Australia*, a Canadian Pacific liner, which was chartered and redesignated as a "royal yacht" for the occasion. The *Repulse* would nevertheless still accompany them halfway across the Atlantic. Naval authorities were worried that the liner might be intercepted by the German battleship *Deutschland*, which was cruising in Spanish waters, leaving the King and Queen in danger of capture.

There followed a frantic operation in which some five hundred men worked day and night to prepare the ship. It was repainted both inside and out, and separate royal suites, each with a drawing room, bedroom and veranda overlooking the sea, were created: the King's on the port side, the Queen's on the starboard. The smoking room was turned into a private dining room, in which was placed the King's plain mahogany dining table, set for sixteen people.

Special fittings and furniture were brought from the royal yacht, *Victoria and Albert*, which was lying at Portsmouth, and provisions for the royal table were sourced: among them were wines from the cellars of Buckingham Palace, pigeons flown in by plane from Bordeaux, a hundredweight of Wiltshire bacon and fifty live crabs. The Queen brought along forty trunks, containing sixty different dresses and ensembles, the details of which had been kept secret. Before leaving on the tour, she had warned the dressmaker that if any details were leaked to the press, she would cancel the order. The King made do with a more modest wardrobe – which, among the various pieces of formal and informal wear, contained three different uniforms: those of Admiral of the Fleet, Field Marshal and Marshal of the Royal Air Force. A new crew had to be recruited and taught the strict rules of royal protocol. As one contemporary observer noted, "When the King travels by sea he does not dispense with the formalities of the royal household."[1] All was done secretly under the supervision of Special Branch officers.

The King, meanwhile, had been making preparations of his own. There had been some discussion as to whether Logue should accompany him on the trip, which was to contain some important speeches – chief among them one to be delivered in Winnipeg on Empire Day. As had been the case with his visit to Australia in 1927, it was decided that the King would manage without his speech therapist – which was fine by Logue. "My wonderful patient goes on wonderfully well, and should have a marvellous time in Canada," he wrote to his brother-in-law, Rupert. "Don't think there is any need for me to go."[2]

The King was nevertheless keen for some advice, and so, the day before departure, Logue was summoned to

Buckingham Palace to run through the speeches he was due to make in Canada. "The King did them splendidly," Logue recorded in his diary. "If he does not get too tired I am certain he will do wonderfully well. As I was going, I wished him all sorts of good luck and he thanked me and said, 'Many thanks Logue, for all your trouble, I am very lucky to have a man who understands voices and speeches so well.'"

Led by the *Repulse* and another escort ship, the *Empress of Australia* reached the open channel around the Isle of Wight by 5 p.m., from where it was seen off by two lines of seventeen ships of the Home Fleet that had come to do the farewell honours. A band aboard the *Rodney* played the national anthem, the warship fired salvoes and a squadron of Royal Air Force planes came swooping down, dipping their wings in a salute.

By 6.30 p.m. the review was over, the liner increased its speed to seventeen knots, and the King and Queen, who had been watching proceedings from the bridge, went to their cabins. Later, as the sun was setting over a tranquil sea, they dined quietly with members of the royal suite, and afterwards listened to a concert of light music played by the ship's eleven-member orchestra. "The ship is quite comfortable, the food is good, but there are too many stewards & liftboys & messengers about – one falls over them at every turn," the Queen wrote to her mother. "But they are so obliging & eager to do anything that we haven't the heart to send them away, poor things."[3]

The King settled down to work, dealing with the state messages received through the radio room, while the Queen got down to some reading, including, surprisingly, Hitler's *Mein Kampf*. "It is very soap-box, but very interesting," she wrote to Queen Mary. "Have you read it Mama?"[4] There were also cinema shows in the main dining room, which the King and Queen attended almost every day, together with those members of the ship's company who were not on duty; at times there were as many as 350 of them. The royal couple so enjoyed *Polar Trappers*, a Donald Duck cartoon set at the South Pole released the previous year, that they had it shown twice in the same week.

The weather quickly took a turn for the worse: early on the 8th, they ran into a belt of fog, rendering the escort vessels almost invisible and forcing the captain to slash the speed; it lifted later that day, only to be replaced by strong winds. The next day, the *Repulse* turned for home, taking back with it mail – among which was a short note penned by the Queen to Princess Elizabeth. "I hated saying goodbye to you & Margaret but know that you will be happy with Miss C [Marion Crawford, their governess] and Alah [Clara Knight, their nanny]," she wrote. "Goodbye my Angel, give Margaret a HUGE kiss, & an ENORMOUS one for yourself from your very loving Mummy."[5]

By then, a half-gale was blowing, giving the *Empress* a serious battering. "Sometimes she would sweep upwards, hover for a moment in the air, and come down into the sea again with a crash," described Gordon Young, a correspondent for the Reuters news agency, one of the three journalists on board who turned his account of the royal tour into an instant book. "The next moment another great wave would seem to knock her sideways. After each battering she would lie still in the sea for a few moments, as though recovering from the shock. Then up she would go again and come crashing down into the sea."[6]

There was worse to come: by the 11th, the wind had given way to thick fog, and the ship's wireless began to receive reports of icebergs. The captain cut the speed to five knots and then stopped completely. The *Empress* was at a standstill for almost twenty-four hours, before finally getting under way again. Then, the next day, three sharp blasts on the ship's whistle announced a sudden reversal in the engines. The lookout had spotted an iceberg straight ahead. A slight rift in the fog revealed whole fields of them on the starboard side, an alarming sight given that it was close to this spot that the Titanic had gone down in 1912. Yet the royal couple seemed remarkably unfazed. "It's almost like being an Arctic explorer," observed the Queen as she watched the icebergs drift past.[7]

"You can imagine how horrid it is," she wrote in a letter to Princess Elizabeth.

One cannot see more than a few yards, and the sea is full of icebergs as big as Glamis, & things called "growlers" – which are icebergs mostly under water with only a very small amount of ice showing on the surface. It is very cold – rather like the coldest, dampest day at Sandringham – double it and add some icebergs, & then you can imagine a little of what it is like. We are all trying to behave like Guides & "smile under difficulties" – and as whatever the conversation [it] usually comes back to ice & god, it gets a little worn sometimes.[8]

Sailors on board described the fog and ice as the worst they had encountered in twenty years, and the ship was falling behind, causing potential havoc with the tightly timed schedule of the royal visit. But the captain, A.R. Meikle, a veteran of many an Atlantic crossing, was not taking any chances. As Young noted drily, another person who must have "felt a special interest in our progress through the ice region" was William Lucas, a bedroom steward, who had been among the survivors of the *Titanic* disaster.[9]

With the ice floes bumping and scraping against the side of the hull, Meikle reluctantly changed course southwards on the morning of the 14th, pointing the ship in the direction of Florida. It proved a wise decision: by that afternoon, they had finally passed the worst of the weather and were able to turn again and head back full speed towards Canada. Early the next day, they finally spotted land – the islands of Saint Pierre and Miquelon, the last relics of the French empire in North America. Aircraft were sent from Southampton and Glasgow to report on ice conditions in the St Lawrence River. Everything was fine.

Escorted by two Canadian destroyers, they made their way at a steady nineteen knots along the river, dropping anchor off the Île d'Orléans, three miles east of downtown Quebec City on the evening of the 16th – two days behind schedule. "I am afraid the Press will have made the most of our eventful voyage to Canada," the King wrote to his mother. He, however, seemed to have remained quite unperturbed by the icebergs. "As a matter of fact I have been able to have a good rest on the voyage, & the two extra days are all to the good for me, but I should not however have chosen an ice field surrounded by dense fog in which to have a holiday, but it does seem to be the only place for me to rest in nowadays!!"[10]

While the King and Queen were at sea, a storm of another sort was brewing – courtesy of the Duke of Windsor, whose presence was to loom over the trip just as it did over most of what his younger brother did during the first years of his reign. The Duke had already provided ammunition for his critics with his visit to Germany eighteen months earlier. On 8th May, after a tour of the battlefields outside Verdun, scene of some of the bloodiest fighting of the First World War, he made a broadcast on America's NBC network – the first such public speech since his farewell message from Windsor Castle on 11th December 1936.

Speaking "simply as a soldier of the last war" and making clear his views did not reflect those of the British government, the Duke voiced a vigorous warning to the world against the horrors of another such conflict. "I break my self-imposed silence now only because of the manifest danger that we may all be drawing nearer to a repetition of the grim events which happened a quarter of a century ago," he said. "The grave anxieties in which we now live compel me to raise my voice in expression of the universal longing to be delivered from the fears that beset us and to return to normal conditions."

No one wanted war, the Duke continued – the Germans as little as the British and the French – but the world seemed to be drifting inexorably towards it. For that reason, statesman should act as "good citizens of the world, not only as good Frenchmen, Italians, Germans, Americans or Britons"; he also urged the discouragement "of all that harmful propaganda which, from whatever source it comes, tends to poison the minds of the people of the world".[11]

The ten-minute speech, which the Duke revealed later he had written himself with the help of the Duchess, struck a chord: after the broadcast, the couple appeared at a third-storey window of the building from which it had been transmitted to receive the cheers of the crowd. He was soon inundated with letters of appreciation, from listeners not just in America but also in France, Holland and Poland, where the speech had been relayed. They came from Britain too, even though the BBC, on the advice of the Palace, had decided not to carry his words. (Britons who wanted to hear the broadcast had to tune their radios to the French broadcast or to the shortwave one from America, although the newspapers printed extracts from it.)

The contents were innocuous enough, a reflection of the Duke's naive hope that, even at this stage, war might yet be averted. For critics, he was misguided to make any equivalence between the attitudes of Britain and France, on one side, and Germany and Italy on the other. The timing, too, was deemed unfortunate. The *Daily Mail* commended the BBC's decision not to carry the speech, saying "a broadcast of the Duke's voice so soon after the departure of the King might have led to entirely false assumptions". It added: "The issue would probably not have presented itself as a delicate problem if the court had been in London." America's United Press news agency, meanwhile, said it seemed as if the Duke were "beginning to act up as soon as the King is out of the country".

The reaction in the Palace to the Duke's proposals was even more critical. Alexander Hardinge, the King's private secretary, found "the idea that it can possibly do the slightest good simply ludicrous". The King's brother, the Duke of Kent, was scathing: "What a fool he is and how badly advised; and everyone is furious he should have done it just before you left," he wrote to the King. "If he had mentioned you in it, it wouldn't have been so bad."[12]

Chapter 7

Westwards through Canada

At 10.35 a.m. on 17th May 1939, George VI landed at Wolfe's Cove, Quebec, becoming the first reigning monarch to visit the North American continent. The previous evening, word had got round that the ship had finally arrived, and tens of thousands of Canadians hurried to the banks of the St Lawrence to be in a prime position to see the royal couple disembark the next morning. They were joined by several thousand Americans from across the border.

They parked their cars and opened their picnic baskets, and soon the pop of corks mingled with the music from radios and portable gramophones. As dawn broke, hundreds of recumbent forms could be seen wrapped in blankets against the cold. Fires were lit as people brewed themselves early-morning tea. In Quebec City itself, men with hoses washed the streets that several hours later would be traversed by the royal motorcade. Flags and bunting taken inside overnight in case of rain were hung out again.

The *Empress of Australia*, looking a little the worse for wear after the battering it had received from the icebergs, was coming to life too. Watched through binoculars by people on the shore, sailors began washing down the decks, while plumes of smoke rose from the chimneys of the escorting destroyers as their stokers got busy. Then, just after 9.30 a.m., a murmur of excitement went through the crowd as the royal liner weighed anchor and began to steam the last short distance to the landing stage. The crowds were swelled by children given the day off from school. Almost everyone was waving small Union Jacks, although here and there they were joined by French tricolours.

Bands played and the bells of every church in the city rang out; car horns added to the cacophony. Gathered on the red carpet laid on the quayside was a host of officials, many in uniforms glittering with gold braid and medals. The civilians wore silk hats. Then came the moment they had all been waiting for: over the side of the handrails on the promenade deck came a glimpse of the cocked hat of an admiral of the fleet, followed by a flash of dove grey. Seconds later, the King and Queen came into full view. Pandemonium broke out below: shouts of "God save the King" mingled with "*Vive le roi*" echoed along the dock and were taken up all along the St Lawrence. The Queen, smiling, waved to the cheering crowd. The King, according to one observer, "looked on with an expression of rather surprised fascination on his face – wondering, no doubt, at the warmth of welcome from people who, up until then, had only read about him and seen his photograph in the papers".[1]

Sword in hand, the King waited at the head of the gangplank for the arrival of Mackenzie King, who was looking resplendent himself in the gold-braided and plumed hat of a member of the Privy Council. The two men talked for a few moments and then, as bugles rang out, the King walked down the ramp and placed his right foot on Canadian soil. A moment later the Queen did the same. The crowds cheered, a twenty-one-gun salute was fired from the Citadelle overhead, and for the first time the national anthem was played in Canada in the presence of the monarch it honoured.

After being formally presented with some fifty people, from the lieutenant governor of Quebec and the mayor downwards, the King and Queen set off aboard an open-top Chrysler car that was equipped with large plate-glass screens and special gearing allowing it to travel at a steady eight miles an hour. Their destination was Quebec's legislative chamber, where dozens of provincial governors, privy councillors and other officials were gathered around two red-draped thrones. At a formal lunch in the Château Frontenac, one of the most famous and beautiful hotels in Canada, Mackenzie King spoke of his pride "to feel that in the person of the King we have among us the living presence of the head of the whole Empire". In his reply, the King spoke of the historic nature of the visit. After a celebratory banquet for 175 people the royal couple settled down in the Citadelle for their first night.

For the next three weeks the King and Queen's home was not to be a hotel but a train, the *Royal Blue*, so called because of the colour of its coaches, a miniature Buckingham Palace on wheels that was to transport them three thousand miles westwards across Canada – and then back again. Large floodlights on the roof ensured it would be clearly visible to the crowds who would turn out at the remotest spots at night to watch it steam across the Prairies.

The King and Queen travelled in the two coaches at the back, known as Cars 1 and 2, with the royal coat of arms in gold below the windows. Car 1 had two main bedrooms, with dressing rooms and private baths, a sitting room for the King and Queen and two bedrooms for members of the royal staff. Car 2 contained another large sitting room, an office, an oak-panelled dining room, two additional bedrooms and a bathroom. There were also dressing rooms for the various uniforms the King would have to juggle during the trip and for the Queen's many costumes.

The Queen's suite, with its blue-grey painted walls and dust-pink damask coverings and curtains, was reminiscent of a country cottage. The King's was done in blue-and-white glazed chintz. Whenever they wanted to check any detail of the trip they had only to pull down a set of specially designed wall maps that ran up and down like blinds. Golden telephones in all of the coaches allowed the royal couple to speak to any member of their entourage they wished. Almost daily these would be wired up to allow them to speak by radio telephone to the princesses Elizabeth and Margaret Rose back home in

England. Both trains had air conditioning, an innovation that had come in only a few years earlier. At each major stop, gangs of workers would pile huge blocks of ice into containers through which air was drawn to be cooled and cleaned.

Nearly five hundred people in total were employed on the train during its journey. Many of them were involved in catering, which proved a massive undertaking: meat, vegetables and fresh fruit were taken on board at stopping points along the line. The milk was specially pasteurized and sealed with caps stamped "Royal Train". Others worked in its Royal Post Office, which dealt with the dozens of letters sent every day by people on board to their friends. Such was the demand for its cancellation mark, "ROYAL TRAIN – CANADA", that their friends would send them packets of envelopes to be posted by the train. Whenever it stopped, passers-by would stuff more letters and postcards into the hands of those on board. It was claimed that as many as two hundred and fifty thousand letters left the train in one day alone. Its staff also had to deal with the hundred or so pieces of mail sent every day to the King and Queen by well-wishers.

The amount of preparation had been considerable: in the weeks before the couple arrived, a full rehearsal had been carried out, during which the train had been sent along the planned route and every inch of the track inspected. The kitchen staff practised using its facilities to prepare meals, and the radios were tested.

In a foretaste of what was to become standard practice on modern royal tours, particular importance was given to the media. The royal train was preceded by half an hour by a separate pilot train that was to be home to 114 reporters, photographers and technicians, mostly from Britain, Canada and America. A press office on board the train was in continuous operation; every hour bulletins were put on noticeboards containing the latest news from the royal train. At each major stopping place, they were issued with a press pack with all the information they needed. In the major cities, they would find a press room, complete with desks, typewriters and cable facilities already set up for them.

The man with the unenviable task of presiding over them – and making sure no one got left behind along the way – was Walter Scott Thompson, a veteran British-born journalist whose first major assignment had been covering Queen Victoria's funeral and who had long since moved to Canada. The pilot train was also home to a contingent of Mounties, who filled an entire car, and were responsible for protecting both trains from undesirable boarders.

The train pulled out of the station at 8.30 a.m. on 18th May. The first short stop was Three Rivers (known today as Trois-Rivières), birthplace of the Hudson's Bay Company, and then it was on to Montreal, where the King and Queen set off on a three-hour, twenty-four-mile drive through the city and its suburbs – passing along the way a temporary camp, complete with totem poles, set up by the Iroquois under the leadership of Chief Poking Fire on the front lawn of one of the grander houses.

Montreal, the capital of French-speaking Canada, was an important stop. As war in Europe loomed, there was rivalry between the English and French speakers about what Canada's stance should be in a forthcoming conflict: while the English speakers seemed disposed to help the Motherland, the French Canadians felt they should avoid entanglements unless Canada itself was attacked. The tumultuous reception both groups gave to the royal pair, however, appeared to have an important psychological effect. As one contemporary observer put it: "The royal pageantry – to which the people of Great Britain are more or less accustomed – came as a thrilling experience to them and has made many of them believe that after all they, as British subjects of the Crown and of the smiling couple they cheered on this day, belong to the Empire which has so long held itself intact."[2]

Ottawa, where the train arrived early the next morning, was just as significant a stop, even though it suffered the brunt of the delay in the crossing, with the time the royal couple were to spend in the city cut from four days to two. Protocol dictated that, with the monarch in residence, the Canadian capital became also the temporary capital of the British Empire. As the driving force behind the trip, Lord Tweedsmuir was the first to greet the King and Queen as the train pulled up at a specially built and ornamented platform on Island Park Drive to the sound of what was to become a familiar twenty-one-gun salute. As befitting the city's status, the royal couple travelled not in the usual open car but instead in an open horse-drawn carriage, accompanied by steel-helmeted troopers, reminiscent of the Household Cavalry. Dressed in the uniform of a field marshal, the King sat in his carriage bolt upright, watched by an enthusiastic crowd estimated as larger than the entire normal population of Ottawa.

For the first time in Canadian history, the Royal Standard was unfurled. The King also had the opportunity to exercise his constitutional role: seated on a scarlet throne in the Senate, he gave royal assent to a bill just passed by Parliament to provide training for Canada's unemployed youth. Although the King was born on 14th December, this day – 20th May – was chosen as his official Canadian birthday. It was in Ottawa, too, that the King and Queen held their first press conference – even though it was rather different in nature from those held by Roosevelt and other American presidents. To start with, rather than be notified by teletype, journalists were sent gilt-edged, engraved cards bearing the Royal Arms of England, the kind of invitation you would receive for a state ball. It was also "suggested" that formal dress would be appropriate.

Then, when the journalists – some in morning coats and striped trousers, and a few rather self-consciously in tweeds

– arrived, they were formed into a circle around the reception room, and the King and Queen passed along, shaking each of them by the hand. To their surprise, they found the royal couple asked them almost as many questions as they put to them. The event nevertheless had the desired effect, generating extensive coverage in both Canada and America, as well as back in Britain.

The readiness of the royal couple to talk caught the imagination of the popular papers in particular. One New York reporter had his hand, which the King had shaken, photographed, and his editor printed it life-size across the front of the paper. The reporter announced he was going to have a plaster cast made of it so he could present it to the Smithsonian Institute. The King was amused by the cuttings when a collection was given to him: seeing an article on the front page of the *New York Daily News* headlined "News Reporter Gabs with the King", he asked that it be kept in the royal archives as a souvenir of the tour.

The royal couple's decision to cultivate the press – and their success in so doing – played an important part in preparing the ground for the short but crucial American part of their trip, on which, because of continued political tensions, there was no guarantee they would receive the warm welcome they were given in Canada. In the months before the visit, the US newspapers' enthusiasm at the forthcoming visit had been tempered with concerns, fuelled by the isolationists, about the nature of the demands that the British might be about to make on them. Typical was an article that appeared in the *New York Daily News* on 9th May. "Their Majesties are guests in our house, and, as such, entitled to the courtesies due to any guest," the paper wrote. "Anything like jeering or even a pronounced silence, when the King and Queen pass through the streets would be highly impolite. They ought to receive, at the least, polite applause." It went on to add: "We should not forget, however, that the King and Queen are not coming over to see us simply because they love us. They are coming here to sell us a bill of goods; to convince us that our interests are identical with theirs."

The newspaper was also unhappy about the haughty manner in which the British embassy was handling preparations for the visit: such as the order by the ambassador's wife to the American press that journalists were not to attempt to talk to the King and Queen unless spoken to first, and the instructions sent to Eleanor Roosevelt telling her how the royal couple liked their beds made up. "As for Their Majesties, they will have a much more auspicious American trip if word can somehow be got through to them to call off sundry officious know-it-alls now misrepresenting them in Washington, and put some reliable American public-relations gent on the job, who understands how to cultivate American public opinion."

In an article a few days later in *The Spectator*, Erwin D. Canham, a prominent American journalist who had spent years working in Britain, took up the argument, blaming such views on the failure of the government in London to explain the purpose of the visit. "Is it principally [...] to emphasize with courtesy and dignity the proper and peculiar place of the United States in relation to the nations – beginning with Canada – over which these rulers reign?" he asked. "Is it, at base, to counteract the after-effects of the abdication and its special relationship to the United States? Can it be stated candidly that the visit really has nothing to do with the present games of power politics?" Canham concluded it was ultimately more to do "with the fundamental long-term relations of our two countries than [...] with the crises of the last nine months", but pointed out that it would have been helpful for a "responsible authority" to spell this out. Otherwise there was a danger the American public would jump to the wrong conclusion.[3]

Such comments touched a nerve back in the Foreign Office, where there was concern about Ronald Lindsay's handling of the American media in the run-up to the royal visit. A note drawn up by one diplomat commenting on the articles in the *New York Daily News* and *Spectator* complained about a "whispering campaign, which is evidently growing in intensity" about the motives for the trip. "Why cannot the simple fact be stated that the one and only occasion for their visit is the invitation issued by the President as soon as he heard that Their Majesties were going to Canada?" he demanded, with an air of exasperation. "I can understand that the US authorities may find advantage in a policy of inactivity as regards these misconceptions; what I cannot understand is that the Embassy should apparently be doing nothing to check their growth". Something had to be done, he concluded, even though "the manner in which the truth should be conveyed to the world will require careful consideration".[4]

Yet, despite continued mutterings from the isolationists, such concerns turned out to be largely misplaced. The more the American papers saw of the royal couple as they followed them around Canada, the more they came to treat the King and Queen as human beings rather than symbols of an outmoded institution or representatives of a country with which they had countless differences. It helped that in person they came across as warm and surprisingly relaxed rather than stiff and formal. The coverage often showed a sense of fun: on 19th May a number of newspapers mischievously published a photograph on their front pages of the King at the official luncheon held for him in Quebec in which he was "apparently weary and on the verge of dozing".

The goodwill seemed mutual. In a letter to her mother-in-law, the Queen, no great lover of the British press, gave her impressions of the correspondents covering them. "They are really very nice, and were so shy and polite," she wrote. "The Americans are particularly easy and pleasant and have been amazed I believe at the whole affair. Of course they have no idea of our Constitution or how the Monarchy works, and were surprised & delighted to find that we were ordinary & fairly polite people with a big job of work."[5]

And then it was on to Toronto, into which they steamed at 9.29 a.m. on 22nd May. There were the usual formal meetings and unveilings – chief among them the inauguration of the Queen Elizabeth Way, a highway linking Ontario's capital with Buffalo in New York State. There was also one of the oddest episodes of the royal visit: a meeting with five four-year-old girls who had arguably been the most famous babies in the world. The Dionne quintuplets – or just "the Quints" as they were known – were born in May 1934, two months premature, just outside Callander, Ontario. The first quintuplets to survive infancy, they swiftly became celebrities. After four months with their family, they were made wards of the King for the next nine years under the terms of a specially passed piece of legislation, the Dionne Quintuplets' Guardianship Act, 1935, and went to live in a specially built nursery across the road from the farmhouse where they were born. There they were cared for by a Dr Allan Roy Dafoe, who became something of a celebrity in his own right.

As the royal visit had drawn closer, there had been intense speculation, not just in Canada but in the United States too, as to whether the royal couple would grant an audience to "the Quints". When the initial itinerary was published and did not include a stop-off in Callander, Dafoe denounced the omission as an "insult to the French-Canadian race", but he and the Quints' parents were mollified when it was announced in March they would be invited to meet the King and Queen in Toronto instead.

In the weeks that followed, the newspapers carried detailed reports on how the five girls were being prepared for their audience – and in particular how they were being taught to curtsy, with Dafoe playing the part of the King during their rehearsals. This proved a particular challenge in the case of Emilie, who had acquired a reputation as the most mischievous of the five and, true to type, caused concern by insisting on performing her curtsy while standing on her head. The five were said to have been disappointed that the King and Queen were not accompanied by their daughters – although it was decided they should bring along a signed photograph of themselves to be passed on to Elizabeth and Margaret Rose.

A week before their fifth birthday, the Quints left their nursery and set off together with their parents, Dafoe and two nurses, aboard a special crimson-and-gold train sent by the Canadian government – dubbed the "Quintland Special" – bound for Toronto and their royal meeting. The five were all dressed up in new white organdie dresses with shiny black patent-leather shoes. In their hair they had rosebuds of different colours so they could be told apart from each other. It was the first time they had ever been more than a hundred yards from the place of their birth, let alone set foot on a train.

A cheer went up in the usually sombre Legislative Assembly of Ontario when the girls arrived, Emilie provoking laughter by trying to wave and bow to everyone present and almost toppling over in the process. Then they were led by Dafoe and their nurses into the formal drawing room to await their audience. When the King and Queen walked in, they were presented first with the adults and then with the Quints, who had been sitting quietly in a row on a couch. They clambered down and walked towards the royal couple, sinking together into perfect curtsies and, one by one, handed the Queen their little bouquets, except for Marie, who insisted on giving hers to the King.

Forgetting what they had been told, Cecile then toddled towards the Queen, holding up her arms. When the Queen bent down, they all embraced her, and what had started as a formal occasion turned into a group hug. Dafoe was delighted. "I had a lump in my throat as big as an apple," he said afterwards. "We had been expecting a sober, formal presentation. What we got was the meeting of a mother and father who had been separated from their own babies, with five little children who, incidentally, happened to be their wards. Believe me, it was the big moment of my life, and the King and Queen were just as thrilled as I was."[6]

From Toronto the train continued westwards to Winnipeg, where it arrived on 24th May. The visit had been overshadowed by news from London that a car carrying Queen

Mary had overturned after colliding with a two-ton truck in Putney in the south-west of the capital. She escaped with only minor injuries. "Bertie and I were deeply concerned when we heard the news of your horrible accident," the Queen wrote a few days later to her mother-in-law. "It must have been absolutely terrifying, and thank God nobody was very badly hurt. You would have been touched to hear of all the anxious inquiries from all sorts & kinds of people here. At little wayside stations, Lord Mayors, politicians, everybody wanted to know how you were getting on."[7]

Some hundred thousand people – including what were thought to be fifty thousand Americans – turned out to catch a glimpse of the royal couple. Despite the day's record rainfall, the King insisted that the convertible roof of their limousine be opened to give the crowd a better view. Among the more curious of the day's royal engagements was a stop at Fort Garry, since turned into a park, where they took part in the unique ceremony of receiving rent from the head of the Hudson's Bay Company, founded in 1670. Under the rules, two elk heads and two rare black beaver pelts were to be paid by the trading company whenever the monarch or his heirs visited its domain.

It was Empire Day, and it had been decided that the King should mark the occasion with a speech on CBC, the Canadian broadcaster, the first to be sent transmitted around the world by a British monarch away from the United Kingdom. At eight hundred words, it was also to be the longest broadcast the King had ever made – no small feat considering his continued aversion to public speaking. In charge of the arrangements was Charles Jennings, a senior CBC broadcaster, whose son, Peter, went on to become a famous news anchor for America's ABC network. Jennings and his technicians set up a temporary studio in the library on the first floor of Government House, where two gold-plated microphones were positioned on a mahogany table. Before the broadcast they all chatted, and a radio was installed in an adjacent bedroom so the Queen could listen to her husband's speech. Jennings described it as "probably the most intimate two hours that the King and Queen have had since they came to Canada".[8]

When the time came for the broadcast, everyone else left, leaving the King alone with Alan "Tommy" Lascelles, his private secretary. In his speech, clearly written with the American leg of his tour in mind, the King extolled "the faith in reason and fair play" that he said was shared not just by Britain and Canada but also by America. "Canada and the United States have had to dispose of searching differences of aim and interest during the past hundred years, but never has one of these differences been resolved by force or threat," he said. "No man, thank God, will ever again conceive of such arbitrament between the people of my Empire and the people of the United States." The speech ended with an appeal to young people. "It is true – and I deplore it deeply – that the skies are overcast in more than one quarter at the present time," he said. "Do not on that account lose heart. Life is a great adventure, and every one of you can be a pioneer, blazing by thought and service a trail to better things."[9]

Jennings described the King's performance as "magnificent" and said the monarch had been suitably impressed with himself. "He came out afterwards, as pleased as a child, saying 'well, the operation's over and it was successful',", Jennings wrote in a letter home.[10] Logue, listening avidly to his pupil back in London, was equally impressed and sent Lascelles a telegram. "Empire Broadcast tremendous success, voice beautiful, resonant speed, eighty minimum atmospheres. Please convey congratulations loyal wishes to His Majesty."[11]

The mood changed as the King and Queen continued westwards: there wasn't a silk hat in sight when on 25th May the *Royal Blue* train arrived at Regina, capital of the wheat-growing province of Saskatchewan. Here, as elsewhere in the Prairies, many people had travelled hundreds of miles by car, by horse-drawn cart or in the saddle in order to get a view of the royal visitors. And then it was on to Calgary, where ninety per cent of the early pioneers came from north of the Tweed, something that endeared the population to the Queen. Here there was a meeting with three hundred Native Americans. The King had been automatically made Big White Chief by a group who had come to London to attend the coronation two years earlier; this counted as a return visit. The spectacle was necessarily somewhat artificial: most of those taking part were normally seen in dungarees and cloth caps rather than elaborate costumes, but it didn't seem to matter.

The scenery changed as they left the Prairies behind and the royal train began to climb into the Rockies, coming to a halt at the pretty, tree-encircled station of Banff at 7.30 p.m. on 27th May. Half an hour later the royal couple were comfortably installed in their own private suite in the Banff Springs Hotel, one of the most expensive and luxurious in Canada. The plan was for an informal weekend, governed by a gentlemen's agreement between royal couple and journalists that, in the years to come, was to become standard practice on such tours. The deal was that the King and Queen would take part in one photo opportunity, and regular updates on their activities would be released. In return, their privacy would be respected. The next day, both the royal couple and the journalists went sightseeing; often someone taking a photograph of the magnificent scenery would see the Queen standing by their side, doing the same. The King, meanwhile, wearing tweeds or shorts and a jacket, set off on long walks, his beloved cine camera in hand.

Such informality made for some curious moments, such as when the Queen found a female American reporter practising a curtsy in front of a mirror. To her surprise, the Queen then took her by the hand and insisted that they practise together. "Can there ever have been such a paradoxical scene – an American girl reporter being taught the curtsy by the royal lady for whom she was learning this feminine mark of respect?" asked Keith V. Gordon, a reporter who wrote a book about the trip.[12]

The next day, a Sunday, they attended the morning service at the Banff Anglican Church, which was so tiny that there was only room for the royal party. The service over, they went on a fifty-mile drive through the mountains to Field, in British Columbia, where the royal train was waiting for them. Unfortunately, some members of the entourage left the hotel so late that when they arrived the train had already departed. The only solution was to charter a bus, in which they then set off on a race through mountain roads. "Those who had to make this breakneck journey said afterwards that it was like a shot out of a Wild West film, and the heavy vehicle lumbered and reeled on the edge of precipice roads where the drop was hundreds of feet," commented Gordon.[13] After more than fifty miles, the group on the bus finally caught a glimpse of the blue-and-silver train glinting in the sun. Racing alongside, they made frantic gestures to the driver to stop. Tired, harassed and badly bruised, they climbed aboard, vowing not be left behind again.

Eventually, at 10 a.m. Pacific Standard Time on 29th May, the *Royal Blue* reached Vancouver, where the royal couple were greeted by the cheers of half a million people who had stood for hours waiting for them. The atmosphere was reminiscent of home – not least the accents, which seemed more English than the Canadian one to which they had become accustomed over the previous week. There were cricket fields rather than baseball parks, and the familiar uprights of football goals. The mayor James Lyle Telford, who greeted them at the station, wore insignia and robes similar to those of the Lord Mayor of London. At the door of City Hall, they were met by a man carrying a mace presented three years earlier by the City of London.

That afternoon, the King and Queen boarded the coastal steamer *Princess Marguerite*, bound for Victoria, on Vancouver Island, the westernmost point of their trip. They slept at Government House and spent the next day at official ceremonies as well as sightseeing amid the green fields and well-kept gardens of a town often described in those years as a "bit of England in the Pacific". They slept a second night there and then, the following afternoon, crossed back to Vancouver and on to New Westminster, a city twelve miles away on the banks of the Fraser River. At 3.50 p.m. on 31st May they boarded the royal train. Six minutes later they set off, turning their back on the Pacific shore and embarking on the long trip eastwards that would eventually take them to the United States.

Chapter 8

And Back

Leaving the busy harbour of New Westminster behind them, the King and Queen travelled up the valley of the Fraser River, the source of which lay almost seven hundred miles away among the ice fields of the Rocky Mountains. As they passed in the brilliant sunshine, the shore was lined with little ships covered with flags, their decks crowded with people. An ancient Mississippi paddle boat served as a viewing platform for several hundred more. From there, as darkness fell, the *Royal Blue* train travelled on by way of tunnels and bridges that led through range after range of mountain peaks. Every quarter of a mile or so along the lonely route, watchmen stood with lanterns. Suddenly the train, brilliantly lit and with a searchlight at the front, would appear out of the darkness. A few moments later it was gone again.

Early the next morning, they passed Mount Robson, which, at 12,972 feet, is the highest mountain in the Rockies, stopping briefly to take on water. Then it was on towards Jasper National Park, an area of outstanding natural beauty that spans some four thousand square miles and lies more than 3,400 feet above sea level. They were put up at the

Jasper Park Lodge, a collection of log cabins set in beautiful parkland that formed a luxury hotel run by the Canadian National Railways.

The royal couple were given the Outlook Cabin, which stood somewhat apart from the rest: built entirely of pine logs peeled and varnished to preserve their natural colour, it had room for eight guests and two servants. The King and Queen had never experienced anything quite like it: the floors were covered with bearskin rugs, while curiously shaped pieces of wood were used for lamp standards and to support the beams. Although it was too early in the year for flowers to grow naturally at that altitude, the beds around the cabins had been specially planted with hothouse flowers the evening before they arrived. Several Mounties stood guard at the entrance, where a flagpole had been specially erected: as the royal couple were driven up in their open car, the Royal Standard was hoisted.

Taking a short break from their official duties, they stayed for a day and a half, resting and sightseeing, and visited a local gorge, glacier and beaver dam. Out walking during the day, they came across a bear with her young cub, which the King filmed with his cine camera as it climbed a tree. Another bear was found scavenging for food under the dining car of the royal train and had to be chased away by the guards. That evening, after a quiet dinner for the two of them, the royal couple sat in front of a miniature projector and ran through the footage of their journey the

King had shot so far. He then edited it with the help of one of the hotel porters. It was to be their last moment of tranquillity before they were to start their sea voyage home two weeks later.

While the King was away talking to veterans, Mackenzie King asked the Queen if she had enjoyed the rest. "Rest?" she exclaimed. Mackenzie King thought they had rather overdone all the walking and climbing. "The King looks to me much fresher and more rested than at the beginning of the trip," he wrote in his diary. "The Queen seems a little tired. Does not look it but I can notice she has lost a little of the constant smile which she wore at the beginning."[1]

At 9.30 a.m. on the next day, 2nd June, the royal train pulled out of Jasper station, bound for Edmonton, capital of Alberta, where the now familiar flurry of engagements was squeezed into the period from 3.30 p.m. to 10 p.m. They included a trip to Portage Avenue, one of the strangest streets in the world, a stretch of smooth paving two and a quarter miles long without a single building on either side. The street had been built in the boom years of the early part of the century, but the outbreak of the First World War checked the development of the city. Its main function had since become to serve as a track for roller-skating children, although it was occasionally used as an improvised aeroplane runway: in 1931, Wiley Post and Harold Gatty had made use of it during their record-breaking flight round the world. Two years later, Post had done the same when he repeated the feat solo.

This time, however, Portage Avenue was being employed for a very different purpose. Hoping to cash in on enthusiasm for the royal trip, the enterprising local authority had erected six-tier grandstands with seating for 68,000 people along its length, which it hoped to sell at one dollar each – quite a vote of confidence in the lure of the royal visit, given that the population of the city was just 89,000. Their gamble paid off. The grandstands were packed, the front rows filled with thousands of schoolchildren who broke into loud cheers as the royal party passed. For Mackenzie King it was "the finest sight in the whole trip thus far".[2] The royal couple drove up one side of the avenue to the far end, where there was a display of different types of aeroplane, and then all the way back again.

As they made their way to the legislative buildings, there was a terrible crush at one point when they stopped en route to talk to some patients at a hospital. Mackenzie King was afraid the crowds would get the better of the situation, but they managed eventually to get through. There were more crowds at the railway station to see them off as they left that evening after dinner with members of the provisional government.

There was a similar outburst of popular enthusiasm at the several stops the King and Queen made the following day: at Watrous, a few miles east of Saskatoon, home to only a few hundred people, a crowd of twenty-five thousand turned out, some of whom had travelled hundreds of miles to see the royal couple with their own eyes. Place of honour on the platform was given to a huge stuffed buffalo in a glass case. At another point, where there was only a single grain elevator and water tower, there were eight thousand visitors. One of the journalists on board the pilot train asked one of them how large the local population was. "Why, nobody lives here," came the reply.[3]

The visit scheduled that evening for Melville, a little town of four thousand people located 170 miles farther east, looked like it might be more controversial: many of the locals were originally from Germany, Czechoslovakia or other parts of Eastern Europe, and the town had a reputation for being a "centre for communism". Any concerns proved misplaced: the residents turned out to be just as enthusiastic royalists as everyone else: police estimated the crowd at between forty and fifty thousand, all of them squeezed around a small raised platform onto which the royal couple were to step from the train. To control them there were just two lines of volunteer ex-servicemen and a handful of Mounties.

As the train pulled in, five bands struck up, gigantic spotlights played on the faces of spectators and the sky was lit up by fireworks. What had been intended as yet another of many short, ten-minute appearances turned into something more substantial. As the jubilant crowds chanted "We want the King", "We want the Queen" and "Come down to us, Your Majesties, we love you", the royal couple stepped down from the dais that had been prepared for them and plunged into the middle of the crowd. To the horror of their security detail, they then spent ten minutes edging their way through the lines of people, stopping to chat as they went. The Queen was surrounded by women, some of whom kissed her as she walked past; others held up their babies for her to kiss. The King got his share of kisses too, as well as thumps on the back from burly farmers.

The royal party were surprised by the size of the turn-out. "We found ourselves simply lost in amazement," said Mackenzie King. "I never saw a more radiant look on the face of the Queen. She and the King threw up their hands in acknowledgement of the cheers and welcome given them."[4] Onlookers were impressed to note that, through it all, they retained their quiet dignity. "They dealt with each onslaught on their good nature with the same regal savoir-faire that they would adopt in formally shaking the hand of a uni-formed official," noted Gordon.[5]

The plan had been for them to spend the night on board the train parked in a siding. But it soon became clear to organizers that if they did so then the crowds would stay too. Loudspeakers implored the spectators to go home, but no one showed any sign of intending to do so and therefore, after hurried consultations among railway officials, it was decided the train should set off, go round a curve in the track and then stop a few miles away, out of sight, where the royal couple would have the chance of an uninterrupted night's sleep. The tactic worked: after a tumultuous farewell under a great yellow prairie moon, the crowds gradually dispersed and embarked on the long journey home – though it took three hours for the last car to go.

The next day, a Sunday, included church at the town of Portage la Prairie and a second, unscheduled stop in Winnipeg. During their first visit to the city as they travelled westwards, time constraints had forced them to cancel a planned meeting with a hundred disabled former servicemen. One of the men sent the King a letter pointing out how disappointed they had been, and so he ordered the new stop.

That was not the only change in the itinerary: the next day, learning that they would be passing near to some of the largest nickel mines in the world, the Queen suggested they make an unscheduled visit to Sudbury, Ontario, which lies almost eight hundred miles east of Winnipeg. Telegrams were dispatched from the train to Sudbury, throwing the town into a frenzy of excitement. All work was immediately stopped in the mines of the International Nickel Company of Canada: one of the largest electric lifts in the Frood Mine, the biggest producer of nickel in the world, was hastily polished, and the lift platform, which lay more than two thousand feet below the surface, was whitewashed.

Company police armed with revolvers stood guard over the mine when the royal party arrived just after sunset. The royal couple changed into protective clothing – the King into regulation khaki overalls and the Queen into a special white waterproof silk outfit – and, wearing miners' helmets on their heads, they faced a barrage of photographers as they emerged from the changing room. "I'm afraid this is not a bit stylish," the Queen laughed, as she posed for pictures.[6] All the same, she fixed her helmet at an angle, giving herself something of a jaunty appearance.

Accompanied by the general manager and the general superintendent, they were escorted to the top of No. 3 shaft. They stepped into the cage, which then descended the 2,800-foot shaft at 1,500 feet a minute, making the royal ears pop. From there they boarded one of the trains used by the miners to take them to and from the rock face. Sitting back to back, their legs covered with rugs against the cold, they rode 1,800 feet to a point where two miners, named Hadley and Simpson, were digging into the ore. After an inspection tour lasting forty minutes, the clanging of a bell announced their return to the surface, where they toured the mine head, dodging the clouds of mosquitoes that were typical of the area. The royal couple "both seemed greatly to enjoy the adventure", thought Mackenzie King.[7]

A small group of newspaper reporters from the train had been given permission to accompany the King and Queen down the mine but, just as they were changing, they were told by mine officials they wouldn't be allowed down after all. Nevertheless, one enterprising figure, H.R. Pratt, editor of the *Kent Messenger*, managed to slip through: the mine officials thought he was with the royal party, and the Mounties were convinced he was with a mine official. Afterwards, he shared his scoop with his colleagues.

The Canadian portion of the tour was drawing to a close: after boarding the train, which was waiting at Garson crossing, the King and Queen spent the night at a quiet little station called South Parry. The next day – 6th June, the last before they crossed the border – saw a series of short halts at little towns including Kitchener, which had been known as Berlin before the First World War and was largely populated by people of German origin, who nevertheless gave the royal visitors an enthusiastic welcome.

There were also some unscheduled stops: at Washago, where the train halted at 9 a.m. to take on water, thirty thousand people chanted "We want the King" continuously for three minutes. He dutifully appeared on the back platform to be greeted by a voice from the crowd shouting, "I Ii-ya King?"

"I'm fine," the King called back smiling, apparently now used to the more informal manner in which he was greeted by his Canadian subjects. "And how are you?"[8]

As the train moved off, people broke through barriers that had been specially erected along the track and rang alongside through the swampy ground – splashing in muddy water that sometimes reached up to their knees. One or two stumbled and fell but picked themselves up again and, undaunted, went on running. Finally the train crossed over a bridge and around a curve, and the crowd reluctantly made their way home.

From then it was back through Toronto and on towards the border. That evening, as they passed through the outskirts of Windsor, Ontario, they had the first sight of the skyline of an American city: across the Detroit River were visible the skyscrapers and an electric sign that proclaimed: "Detroit Welcomes Their Majesties the King and Queen". "What a wonderful sight," said the Queen as she and the King stood and looked in awe together.[9]

A foretaste of the reception that they would be given on the other side came when they stopped later in Windsor, where the crowds of locals were joined by some two hundred thousand Americans "in a welcome so uproarious that it almost looked at one time as though the crowd would lift up the royal train and carry it bodily away", as one observer put it.[10] Before crossing into the United States, though, they had another day of visits on Canadian soil: in one of the most gruelling parts of the tour, they were to stop in no fewer than six towns in southern Ontario, each of them packed with crowds of wildly enthusiastic people.

There was also an awkward issue to resolve: Lascelles mentioned almost in passing to the Queen that when they crossed the border, for protocol reasons, they would have to leave behind the Mounties who had been guarding them during the trip. The Queen suddenly became more agitated and assertive than Mackenzie King had seen her for the whole journey, insisting that the Mounties' presence made her feel more secure, and they could not possibly be left behind. The King then weighed in on her side, declaring, "We must have them. We cannot think of going to the States without them."[11] But his aides warned that taking the Canadian police with them might lead to "real jealousies and difficulties", since it would look as if they didn't trust the Americans – a point that could be seized on by the press there. There was talk of taking up the issue with the President, but the King and Queen eventually backed down for fear of causing an incident. It was also pointed out that there wouldn't be enough room on the train for two sets of security to sleep anyway.

They arrived at the Canadian side of Niagara just after 7 p.m., slightly later than scheduled, after being delayed by the thousands of people who turned out to greet them along the route from St Catherine's, the penultimate stop of the day. They viewed the Falls from Table Rock and then went to a small dinner party at the General Brock Hotel, where they stepped out onto the balcony to acknowledge the cheers of ten thousand schoolchildren gathered outside. Later they returned to watch the Falls illuminated by coloured lights.

Then it was a short drive to the station for the brief journey across the border. Despite the past gruelling two days, they seemed cheerful and refreshed. As one admiring correspondent for the *New York Times* remarked, "Fresh as a

debutante before her first big party, Queen Elizabeth wound
up a strenuous day today with her costume as crisp and her
manner as gracious as if she were beginning – instead of
entering the final phase of – her tour."[12]

While the King and Queen had been greeted with enthusiasm wherever they went, security remained a concern,
especially for the next stage of the trip. Since their arrival
in Canada, Chief Constable Albert Canning of Scotland
Yard, who was travelling on board the *Royal Blue* train, had
been watching with concern the progress through America
of Seán Russell, a militant veteran of the 1916 Easter Rising
and Irish Civil War, who the previous year had become chief
of staff of the Irish Republican Army (IRA).

Canning's concern was understandable. On 12th January,
the IRA, under Russell's leadership, had "declared war" on
Britain in the name of the Irish people and given the government in London an ultimatum: pull all British forces out of
Ireland within four days or they would start a campaign to
sabotage the military and commercial life of Great Britain.
The deadline came and went. Four days later came the first
attacks, in London, Warwickshire and Northumberland.
There were dozens more in the months that followed, on
power stations, post offices, banks and railway stations,
not just in the capital but in towns and cities across the
country. Although the IRA's main target was infrastructure,
several people were killed and injured during the campaign,

which was known as the "S-plan" (S for sabotage) and was to continue after the outbreak of war into early 1940. The group's leaders had also started exploring the possibility of establishing links with the Nazis. The government was naturally worried about the possibility of "Irish outrages" in America to coincide with the royal visit.

That April, with the bombing campaign in full swing, Russell had set off to America on a propaganda tour to raise his own profile and that of the IRA. The forthcoming royal visit appeared to provide a potentially valuable opportunity for publicity. Once on American soil, Russell had given a series of inflammatory speeches to his sympathetic Irish-American audience, in which he admitted to ordering the bombings and vowed to continue doing so until British troops left the country and his men were released from jail. "A state of war exists between England and Ireland and will continue until the British troops are withdrawn," he declared.

Unknown to Russell, he was being trailed by American G-men at the behest of Canning (who himself arrived in New York on 20th April, bearing letters of introduction to Lewis J. Valentine, the city's commissioner of police, and J. Edgar Hoover, head of the FBI). They finally sprang into action on 5th June, when Russell boarded a train in Chicago and arrived in Detroit, just over the border from Windsor, the day before the *Royal Blue* train was due to pass. He was arrested by three federal officers as he was about to get into a taxi outside Michigan Central Station and charged with entering the United States illegally.

Joseph McGarrity, from Philadelphia, a leader of an Irish-American society who was with Russell at the time of his arrest, was indignant at his treatment. Speaking to journalists, he denied that he and Russell had any intention of going to Windsor. "As for the visit of the King and Queen, if you read the papers you must know that the Irish Republican Army does not kill people," he declared. "There should be no apprehension there."[13]

Despite the arrest, which was kept quiet by authorities for several hours, journalists covering the trip noticed clear signs that security was being tightened. At Windsor, more guards were in evidence than at any time during the royal trip. Authorities there also accepted an offer from Detroit to supply detectives, who mingled with the crowd. It was the first time US police had ever guarded a British monarch.

Russell's arrest outraged many members of the Irish-American community and culminated in protests by seventy-six members of Congress of Irish descent, who demanded an explanation from Roosevelt and threatened to boycott the King's planned visit to Congress. The police's action nevertheless clearly came as a relief to Canning and his men. Asked if he had any apprehension about security during the American leg of the trip, he replied: "Not so much now."

Chapter 9

An American Obsession

Although George VI was to be the first reigning British monarch to set foot on American soil, he and his family were already familiar figures to American newspaper readers. Princess Elizabeth had proved to be a particular source of fascination: in April 1929, *Time* magazine marked the future queen's third birthday by making "Princess Lilibet" its cover story, even though her father was not even first in line to the throne at the time. The activities of her uncle turned out to be an even bigger story: details of Edward VIII's burgeoning relationship with Wallis Simpson were splashed over the American papers for many months before their self-censoring British counterparts dared to touch the story.

It was all a far cry from the 1770s, when tyrannical King George had been a hate figure for Americans fighting for independence. "George III loomed large in America's foundation myth, and thus became a fixture in United States history, an antitype of the Founding Father," writes Frank Prochaska in *The Eagle and the Crown*, a study of American attitudes to monarchy.[1] Yet, even at the height of the War of Independence, the antipathy was not total. As Prochaska argues, a large number of colonists actually remained sympathetic to the Crown throughout the hostilities. And, as the war receded and relations between the two countries recovered, the King was transformed from tyrant into a harmless curiosity and a source of fascination to America's emerging mass media.

Although Britain and the United States found themselves at war again in 1812, George III's son, the then Prince Regent and future King George IV, largely escaped blame for British aggression; given his obvious lack of interest in affairs of state, it was difficult to hold him personally responsible for his country's foreign policy. American newspaper readers were nevertheless intrigued by his private life, whether the tragic death of his sole heir, Princess Charlotte, in 1817 or the very public and acrimonious break-up of his marriage to Queen Caroline, which was fought out in the newspapers over the following few years in much the same way as the events leading to Prince Charles's divorce from Diana, Princess of Wales, were to be during the 1990s.

The accession of Queen Victoria to the throne in 1837 brought a dramatic change in royal tone, but also a further upsurge of American interest. The sight of the leaders of the most powerful nation on earth paying homage to an eighteen-year-old woman fuelled the imagination. The year after Victoria's coronation it was rumoured that President Van Buren intended to offer her his hand in marriage and had sent his son, John, to England with the formal proposal.

But although the younger Van Buren attended the coronation and even later dined with the Queen, no proposal of marriage was forthcoming.[2] Notwithstanding this disappointment, relations between the two countries went from strength to strength. Victoria, increasingly seen as the embodiment of family and Christian values, became hugely popular on the opposite side of the Atlantic.

It would take a royal visit, though, to take this interest to a new level: in 1860 the royal family obliged – even though it was not to be Victoria, herself, but her eldest son, Albert Edward, the future Edward VII, who did the honours. The eighteen-year-old Prince was due to pay a visit to Canada, aimed at cementing imperial relations and rallying Canadians of different origins to the Crown. When President James Buchanan, known to the royal family thanks to an earlier stint as minister in London, heard about the trip, he wrote to the Queen suggesting that the Prince travel on to the United States, assuring her that he would receive a warm welcome. Victoria agreed.

Journeying aboard the battleship *Nero*, Edward left Plymouth on 10th July, accompanied by a large retinue that included the Duke of Newcastle, the secretary of state for the colonies. They arrived two weeks later in the remote fishing village of St John's in Newfoundland. The Canadian part of the visit was packed with official duties – among them the laying of the foundation stone of the Federal Parliament in Ottawa and the opening of a railway bridge in Montreal

– with countless speeches to be made, inspections to be carried out and meetings to be held. There were some lighter moments too: on the Canadian side of the Niagara Falls, the Prince watched as Charles Blondin, the French acrobat, crossed on a tightrope from America, pushing a man in front of him in a wheelbarrow. Blondin offered to take the Prince on the return trip, and he accepted, only to be told by his aides this was out of the question. So Blondin went back on stilts and the Prince travelled instead to Hamilton, where he opened an agricultural show.[3]

The American stage, during which he covered more than five thousand miles over the course of a month, was far more informal. With no official business, the Prince was free to devote himself to entertainment and sightseeing and generally to fly the flag for the monarchy – which suited him absolutely fine. The Queen had decided that he would travel incognito as Lord Renfrew – the name he adopted when in Europe. But no one was fooled. Edward was received at the White House by Buchanan, the bachelor President, and Harriet Lane, his thirty-year-old niece and First Lady, whom the young Prince thought "a particularly nice person and very pretty".[4]

A visit by the Prince to George Washington's tomb at Mount Vernon was welcomed as a symbolic act of reconciliation between Britain and its former colony. When the Prince travelled on to New York City, an estimated half a million people turned out to see him being driven through the city in a six-horse barouche. The festivities were capped by a grand ball at the Metropolitan Opera House. Some three thousand members of the city's moneyed elite were invited, but five thousand turned up, causing the floor to give way. Carpenters were called, but it took them two hours to repair the damage. When proceedings finally got under way after midnight, the young women vied with each other for the privilege of dancing with the Prince.

Reports of such goings-on were read with some concern by the strait-laced Prince Albert, who warned his son never to forget "how constantly you are watched, observed and described". The Prince retorted: "I am quite aware that I am closely watched and must be careful in what I do." Nevertheless, a few days later the *New York Herald* claimed the Prince had "whispered sweet nothings" to the ladies as he directed them in the dance. "His royal highness looks as if he might have a very susceptible nature and has already yielded to several twinges in the region of his midriff," it reported.[5]

Despite – or rather, because of – such behaviour, the visit turned out to be an undoubted success with the Prince's hosts; the newspapers suggested Victoria encourage her son to take an American bride. "She can never find a friend so valuable or so staunch as the United States, if only she can secure our friendship," said *Harper's Weekly*. "And there is no way so simple – in view of the character of our people – to secure that friendship as by having her Prince marry an American."[6]

Although Edward failed to oblige, the visit undoubtedly gave a boost to relations between the American people and the monarchy. These were to endure the difficulties presented by the Civil War, which began the following year, to a British government determined to stay neutral between the two sides. In the decades that followed, Britain's royalty remained an object of fascination. The American press reported extensively on the events held in Britain and elsewhere in the Empire to mark Victoria's Golden Jubilee in 1887 and Diamond Jubilee a decade later, and numerous celebrations were held across America. When she died in 1901, flags were flown at half mast at the White House while the House of Representatives adjourned in a mark of respect. "It is not for mere show that the Americans have received the news of the death of Queen Victoria as a bereavement of their own and commented upon it in terms such as they would employ in the case of an honoured president dying in office," commented the *Los Angeles Times*.[7]

As King, Edward continued to maintain contacts with America from his visit four decades earlier and, given his interest in foreign policy, played a part in keeping Anglo-American relations good, even though there was no question of his making another trip across the Atlantic. He and President Theodore Roosevelt nevertheless wrote frequently to one another and exchanged gifts; one of Edward's last acts was to approve arrangements for a dinner he was to host for the Roosevelts at Buckingham Palace. He died before it could take place: 20th May 1910, the day on which it was scheduled, was instead the day he was buried after a grandiose funeral ceremony attended not just by nine crowned heads and more than thirty royal princes, but also by thousands of Americans – among them Roosevelt.

The coronation of his son, George V, in June the following year was a major event for the American newspapers, while cinemas showed motion pictures of the occasion. Yet the new king, it quickly became clear, was not especially keen on Americans or indeed on any foreigners, preferring instead the company of his fellow Englishmen. Although he had twice visited Canada during his father's reign, George had never crossed the border, and certainly did not have the intention of doing so now he was king.

His eldest son, the future Edward VIII, was a different matter. Unlike his traditionally minded father, he keenly embraced the new – which had by then become synonymous with America. Over time, his accent began to assume a transatlantic twang, and it was noted that he would eat in the American manner, first cutting up his food and then using only his fork, held in the right hand. In what was ultimately to prove his undoing, he also acquired a liking for American women.

This penchant did not go unnoticed by the American press: "Possibly owing to their democratic bringing up," the *New York Times* commented, "[American women] do not stand in as much awe of royalty, even when it is incarnated in a

stripling, as does the average Englishwoman, whose obse-
quiousness is calculated to make a youth like the Prince feel
uncomfortable."[8] His encounters with American soldiers
in France during the war further fuelled his enthusiasm for
the New World.

In 1919, at the instigation of David Lloyd George, the
Prime Minister, Edward embarked on a series of visits to different parts of the Empire with the aim of bolstering support
for the Crown. The first such trip was to Canada – which so
impressed him that he bought a small ranch in Alberta. After
much cabling backwards and forwards to London, the Prince
obtained permission from his father to travel on across the
border to the United States. It was a mixture of the official –
a visit to President Woodrow Wilson, who had just suffered
a stroke, and the laying of a wreath at Washington's tomb
at Mount Vernon – with the razzamatazz of a ticker-tape
welcome in New York. It was, in many respects, reminiscent
of his grandfather's visit sixty years earlier. In fact, the two
Edwards had much in common: "the same build, the same
mental makeup, and the same taste for brandy and soda,
which presented difficulties in a country with prohibition".[9]

There were also the same attempts by the American press
to set up the Prince with a potential American wife. The visit
even inspired the strangely prophetic romantic comedy, *Just
Suppose*, first a play (1920) and then a film (1926), about a
prince who falls in love with an American girl and offers to
give up his right to the throne in order to marry her.

The crowds loved the Prince, as did the American papers, which warmed to his modernity and lack of stuffiness. Their British counterparts were also impressed, hailing the heir to the throne as a "prince among democrats", "a regular fellow" and a "good little salesman, with winning smiles", who was "prepared to put old prejudices aside and open up a line of credit with his house".[10] The Prince was equally enamoured of what he had seen. America, he was to write in his memoirs, "meant to me a country in which nothing was impossible".[11] George V, already becoming worried about Edward's suitability as his successor, was nevertheless concerned that some of his activities were not commensurate with the dignity expected of the heir to the throne.

Such fears were only underlined by a return visit in 1924. American attitudes towards the Prince had changed in the meantime, with the newspapers full of stories of his romantic adventures. The tone of the coverage was set by the *New York Daily News*, which proclaimed in a front-page headline on 29th August 1924, the day he arrived in New York aboard the liner *Berengaria*: "Here He Is Girls, the Most Eligible Bachelor Yet Uncaught".

The Prince certainly lived up to his louche image, making for Long Island, the setting for F. Scott Fitzgerald's *The Great Gatsby*, which was published the following year although set in 1922. He was the guest of James Burden, a wealthy businessman, and spent most of his time watching the polo while glamorous hostesses vied for his attentions.

The trip became an endurance test "with the bank balances of the refulgent chieftains of the Long Island set pitted against His Royal Highness's health", wrote one gossip columnist under the pseudonym "Cholly Knickerbocker". "Never before in the history of metropolitan society has any visitor to these shores been so persistently and extravagantly feted."[12]

The Prince had a grand old time. "By the time I had to return to Great Britain," he wrote in his autobiography, "I had picked up quite a full line of American slang, acquired a taste for bathtub gin, and had decided that every Briton in a position to do so should make a practice of visiting that great country at least once every two or three years."[13] Yet the American press reports of his goings-on, although much exaggerated, caused consternation back home that the Prince allowed himself to be "surrounded by a group of newly rich social thrusters who exploited him in the most flagrant fashion". It was difficult to persuade ordinary Americans that "the British economic situation requires sympathetic consideration when the life at Long Island is held before their eyes as a symbol of what Great Britain, in its highest expression, delights in".[14]

Reading the newspaper cuttings prepared for him by his officials, George V was predictably alarmed by the potential impact on relations with America, which had been so carefully cultivated since his own father's visit there. The result, according to the Prince, "of all this uninhibited journalism was that my father privately broke off relations between America and the members of his family", placing "a series of vague but irremovable objects" in the path of any attempt by him or his brothers to visit the country.[15]

Yet this did little to dent the Prince's enthusiasm for America – or indeed for American women. The development of his romance with Wallis Simpson – described coyly as his "Friend No. 1" in an article in the *Washington Post* two days after his accession in January 1936 – filled countless column inches. While British readers were kept in the dark, their American counterparts were treated to more and more details of his growing relationship with his twice-married lover; the frenzy hit a peak that summer when the pair set off on a Mediterranean cruise aboard the luxury yacht *Nahlin*. His abdication speech that December was broadcast on hundreds of radio stations; those who missed it – or simply wanted to listen again – could buy a copy on record for a dollar at the department store Macy's.

Americans seemed divided as to whether Edward had been right to follow his heart – or was guilty of putting his own well-being ahead of his duty to country and empire. There was also speculation about how long the relationship could last. "What can she give him to compensate for the Empire he tossed away for her?" asked the *Washington Post*.[16] Yet there was also sympathy for Wallis and speculation that the couple might choose to settle in America.

George VI was clearly a very different character, a point that had been grasped by the American press even before he came to the throne. Although nervous and lacking his elder brother's charisma, they decided, he more than compensated for this with his dedication and solid family background. He was, according to one commentator, who reflected on his "brooding inferiority complex", stammer and poor health, "a perfect example of bulldog grit overcoming terrific obstacles".[17] The King's coronation the following May – held on the same day as Edward had been due to be crowned – proved to be a draw, with as many as twenty thousand Americans making the journey across the Atlantic to attend.

Yet American attitudes to the British monarchy remained ambivalent. While the main appeal lay in the pomp and its other historical trappings, this appeared to be coupled with a desire that the royals should somehow be seen to be ordinary people. This was reflected in a number of the articles that had appeared in the American papers before the visit.

Typical was a report, syndicated by the NEA news service, across the front page of California's *San Jose News* under the banner headline "Americans Will Not Find King and Queen Snobbish". "Some of the false storybook glamour that surrounds royalty in the minds of Americans – the feeling that kings and queens are made of different clay than the corner grocer – may be dispelled by the history-making visit of two modest human beings named King George VI and Queen Elizabeth," it began. "For this first British king and queen to set foot on American soil are simple and personally popular people who are far less likely to 'put on airs' than would many of their snobbish subjects in England's so-called upper classes."[18] The royal couple's hosts were not to be disappointed.

Chapter 10

Towards Washington

The *Royal Blue* train crossed the border and came to a halt on the platform of the Suspension Bridge station, on the American side of the Niagara Falls, at 9.35 p.m. on 7th June. The platform of the dingy little station was only a few yards wide and was filled with a hundred soldiers with fixed bayonets and numerous police. A crowd of onlookers was gathered behind them. On the far side was a stand packed with American photographers, newsreel men and broadcasters.

The train stopped with the royal coach exactly opposite a narrow space on the platform between two lines of soldiers. The King, dressed in a double-breasted suit, was the first to alight, shaking the hand of Cordell Hull, the US secretary of state, almost before Ambassador Lindsay had time to make the formal presentation. The Queen followed shortly afterwards. "Your majesties, on behalf of the government and people of the United States I have the honour and pleasure of extending to you our warmest welcome," declared Hull, smiling cheerfully. "All are delighted with your visit. The people of my country, in the most genuine spirit of cordiality, hospitality and friendliness, have every desire to make your stay a thoroughly enjoyable one."[1]

While the rest of the welcoming committee was being presented to the King and Queen, several other members of the royal party who got off the train from other carriages found themselves trapped on the wrong side of the lines of soldiers, who refused to let them through, obliging them to get back on the train, walk along it and emerge through the last car. The ceremonies over, the King and the rest of the royal party climbed back on board. A roar of welcome went up from the crowd packed outside the station when, at 10.58 p.m., after a fifteen-minute stop, the train steamed out of the station. The pilot train, lengthened by two carriages to accommodate an extra batch of American correspondents, had set off five minutes earlier.

The King and Queen sat looking out of the window at the crowds who had gathered to get a glimpse of them. Some eight thousand troops lined the track between Niagara and their first stop, in Buffalo, twenty miles down the line. Policemen were there too, guarding every bridge, crossing and culvert over which the train passed. Until late in the night, the King spoke to Hull and the other officials. He also held a private investiture in the royal compartment, making Lascelles a Knight Grand Cross of the Royal Victorian Order and Lindsay a Knight Grand Cross of the Order of the Bath. This unusual step was taken so that they would be able to wear their new orders during the trip to Washington. In the smoke-filled pilot train, meanwhile, Michael J. McDermott, the chief of the Division of Current Information in the State Department, who was now in charge of the media, "had the unenviable task of settling to the satisfaction of every correspondent the details of how each event during the four-day visit was to be reported for the world's press".[2]

While the royal couple had been making their progress through Canada, preparations had been continuing for their reception on the other side of the border. Appropriate protocol when it came to relations between monarchy and the republican United States had long been a ticklish matter. Although often in awe of royalist ceremonial, Americans – at least those representing their country in an official capacity – felt that they should not become a part of it, for fear of compromising their egalitarian principles. Under a circular issued by the State Department in 1853, US diplomats abroad were required to wear the plain clothing of an American citizen – even at the Court of St James's, with its complicated dress code. Thus, a series of ambassadors and visiting dignitaries made a point of wearing normal dress when presented to Queen Victoria, even though some, in a nod to etiquette, accessorized it with a sword.

By the time of her great-grandson's visit, attitudes had changed, and America seemed happier to play along with protocol – as was demonstrated by Roosevelt's teasing of Joseph Kennedy and his knee breeches. There was also a clear desire to demonstrate that the country could do ceremonial too. For that reason, the tone of the royal couple's reception at the White House had to be formal, albeit displaying republican rather than royalist pomp. By contrast, the emphasis during the twenty-four hours the King and Queen would spend at Hyde Park was to be on simplicity: when they arrived on the Saturday night they would be guests of honour at an informal dinner for a few people. Then, the next day, after church, there would be a picnic at the President's newly built stone cottage on the top of the hill. According to Eleanor, her husband "always behaved as though we were simply going to have two very nice young people to stay with us".[3]

The Roosevelts already had some experience of European royalty. In the summer of 1938 they had received the Swedish Crown Prince and Princess; the following April their Norwegian and Danish counterparts arrived within a few days of each other. As Eleanor put it in her autobiography: "The people of Europe were deeply troubled by the general feeling of unrest and uncertainty on the Continent and were looking for friends in other parts of the world – hence their sudden interest in the United States."[4] For his part, the President was keen to welcome them: "Convinced that bad things were going to happen in Europe, he wanted to make contacts with those he hoped would preserve and adhere to democracy and prove to be allies against fascism when the conflict came," she wrote.[5]

The pattern for each of the Scandinavian visits was similar: the guests would tour the settlements of their fellow countrymen and then come to Springwood for an informal dinner and picnic at the President's cottage. While Olav and Märtha of Norway made a good impression, Denmark's Crown Prince Frederick did not go down so well with his hosts: he was "more interested in his holiday than in the serious questions of the moment and had perhaps less realization of the menace of Hitler than we had expected of one in his position", Eleanor observed.[6]

The visits had passed off well, but these were merely the heirs to the thrones of small countries. Hosting the King and Queen of the United Kingdom was on a wholly different scale of importance – as Roosevelt himself realized. "No detail of the preparations for the King and Queen was too minute for Father's personal attention," wrote his son, Elliott. With Congress rejecting almost everything he was asking for at the time, masterminding the visit became for the President "a rare form of escape, more enjoyable even than browsing over a stamp collection".[7] This meant drawing up the guest lists and specifying the seating plan for every formal meal with due regard to all the most delicate points of protocol. Roosevelt ordered the bindings for presentation copies of his *Public Papers and Addresses* for the King, while the Queen was to be given a special copy of Eleanor's memoirs, *This Is My Story*.

For the Hyde Park segment of the visit, the President asked the neighbours and his half-brother's cockney widow, Betty, to offer their spare bedrooms to house the British contingent. He also enlisted Henry St George Tucker, the head of the Episcopal Church in the United States, to preach the sermon during the service to which he and Eleanor would accompany the royal couple on the Sunday morning. Edith Helm, Eleanor's social secretary, was "halfway drowned in his memos", the President's son recalled. "Why had Lady Nurnburnholme been omitted from the list for tea? How about Franklin Jr for one of the Hyde Park dinners?"[8] Not even Eleanor could escape. Elliott recalled one occasion on which the President demanded his wife provide him with a list of all the British visitors, all the American officials attached to them, all the families who would be at the picnic and all the members of his and her staff within twenty-four hours so he could work out the invitations for the church service.

While Roosevelt was both amused and impressed by the pomp and pageantry that surrounded royalty, his mother took it all deadly seriously. "To her," said Elliott, "reigning monarchs were among the few people in the world ranking in dignity with herself. Hyde Park became a sort of *petit palais* when royalty visited. She covered the top of her grand piano with rows of their autographed photographs in gilt frames, arranged like a pictorial *Almanach de Gotha*." As a result, as the mistress of Hyde Park, she was in an even "greater tizzy" than the President about the impending visit, and borrowed Betty's best glassware and china. Not so Eleanor: according to her son, "her homespun notions of hospitality extended to the scrambled eggs she prepared for all seasons and square dancing in the East Room of the White House after a simple supper." Yet, inevitably, despite her best efforts, the First Lady could not avoid being carried along with the enthusiasm.[9]

That being said, Eleanor was tickled by what she saw as the ridiculous side of this obsession with protocol – best exemplified by a secret memorandum on the visit sent to her and her husband by William Bullitt, the US ambassador to France. Based on his observation at close hand of the royal couple's visit to Paris, the document went into considerable detail as to how the King and Queen should be received – including the stipulation that a hot-water bottle be put in every bed – which Eleanor dutifully obeyed, although with the temperatures in the mid-nineties during the day, it must have been unbearable. "I still keep that memorandum as one of my most amusing documents," she wrote years later. "Among other things, he listed the furniture which should be in the rooms used by the King and Queen, told me what I should have in the bathroom and even the way the comfortables on the beds should be folded."[10]

Bullitt did not have a monopoly on odd proposals. Even more bizarre was the suggestion by one company that the royal couple would only enjoy their tea if it were made with the same kind of water they had at home. The company

consequently analysed the London water and tried to reproduce it in America, sending Eleanor Roosevelt several bottles
as a sample. After further analysis, it was decided they would
be safer drinking water from the Potomac River, after all.

More serious was the question of security: the people
from Scotland Yard had, of course, to stay in the house;
also, messengers had to sit outside the King and Queen's
respective rooms. Eleanor Roosevelt thought this odd, since
the two rooms were opposite each other across the corridor
and their sitting room was just a couple of steps away. It
was only when she spent two nights in Buckingham Palace
in 1942 and saw how large it was that she understood the
thinking behind the tradition.

A day before the visit, Eleanor Roosevelt invited Lady
Lindsay, the wife of the British ambassador, for last-minute
tips. A fellow American, whom Eleanor had known for some
time, Lindsay had a wicked sense of humour. "Sir Alan
Lascelles has told us that the King must be served at meals
thirty seconds ahead of the Queen," she said. "The King
does not like capers or suet pudding. I told him that we did
not often have suet pudding in the United States and that I
really had not expected the King to like capers."

Eleanor passed on to her husband the instruction that
Fields, the White House head butler, would have to stand
with a stopwatch in hand in order to dispatch the butler to
serve the Queen and herself at precisely the right moment.
He was dismissive – especially since the rule at the White

House was that the President had to be served first. "We will not require Fields to have a stopwatch," Roosevelt replied. "The King and I will be served simultaneously and you and the Queen will be served next."

There were other problems associated with combining the various rules of protocol of the Palace with those of the White House, such as furniture: in the dining room of the White House were two special high-backed armchairs, one for the President and the other for the First Lady, and no one else was allowed to sit there. So what was to be done with the royal visitors? "Why don't we buy two more chairs identical with those we now have?" suggested Roosevelt. The two chairs were duly purchased.

The decision as to where to place these chairs prompted another protocol question: should the President sit with the King on his right and the Queen on his left and Eleanor to the right of the King as might seem most respectful to the royal visitors? It was decided instead that the Queen would sit on the President's right while, on the opposite side of the table, the King would sit on Eleanor's right, on the grounds that the visitors were already going to see a lot of their hosts and this would at least give them the chance to talk to some other people. "Franklin later explained this to the King, who accepted every arrangement in the most charming and delightful manner," she said.

And then there was the question of what entertainment should be offered at the dinner. The general consensus was that they should invite singers from the Metropolitan Opera, but the Roosevelts wanted to put on something the royal visitors would not have at home in England – which meant a festival of American folk art. They nevertheless engaged some well-known artists, too: Lawrence Tibbett was to sing several songs, Kate Smith to perform 'When the Moon Comes over the Mountain', which the King was apparently keen to hear, and Marian Anderson, an African-American contralto, asked to interpret some Negro spirituals and other songs. There were also ballad singers and dancers from the south.

While such discussions were going on within the White House, the press and the public were becoming agitated. Emerging as one of the hottest subjects was the picnic for the royal couple at Springwood, as part of which, it was reported with some excitement, they would be served that most quintessentially American dish: the hot dog.

It was Eleanor Roosevelt who first mentioned the "h-word" during a press conference in Washington on 17th May. She let slip to reporters that a "friendly family argument" was under way over the royal programme at Hyde Park. Her mother-in-law favoured a garden party, she said, while she wanted to hold a picnic – with hot dogs, if the weather were pleasantly cool, but without them if the temperature hit one hundred degrees Fahrenheit (thirty-eight degrees Celsius), in which case "more appropriate refreshments" would be provided.

The prospect of the royal couple being fed such food provoked curiously strong feelings: since its arrival from Germany in the late nineteenth century, the humble hot dog, eaten always by hand and never with a knife and fork, had been transformed into a potent culinary symbol. For many, the idea of the King and Queen enjoying hot dogs alongside their hosts would represent their acceptance of American democratic values; others shared Sara Roosevelt's horror.

"Oh dear, oh dear, so many people are worried that 'the dignity of our country will be imperilled' by inviting royalty to a picnic, particularly a hot-dog picnic," Eleanor Roosevelt wrote in the 26th May edition of 'My Day', her syndicated column.[11]

My mother-in-law has sent me a letter she received, which begs that she control me in some way and, in order to spare my feelings, she has only written a little message on the back: "Only one of many such."

But she did not know, poor darling, that I have received "many such" right here in Washington. Let me assure you, dear readers, that if it is hot there will be no hot dogs, and even if it is cool, there will be plenty of other food, and the elder members of the family and the more important guests will be served with due formality. It might be possible to meet the desire of these interested correspondents if there were not quite so many who berate me for too much formality and too much courtesy. I am afraid it is a case of not being able to please everybody and so we will try just to please our guests.

As far as Eleanor was concerned, what people remembered of a visit abroad were the differences from the way things were done at home – the odder, the better – rather than the similarities. "We certainly don't want to make everything so perfectly English that there will be nothing for our guests to smilingly talk about afterwards," she wrote in a sentence that was actually deleted from her column.[12]

Ambassador Lindsay couldn't dodge the hot-dog question when he gave a press conference on 27th May. Had the King and Queen had ever eaten such an item, he was asked. The ambassador indicated they had probably done so at some time, "but I think it will be the first time they have eaten the things under that name".

"What name have they eaten them under in other circumstances?" demanded one persistent reporter.

"Oh, a rose by any other name would taste just as sweet," the ambassador retorted.

Lindsay also revealed that no changes would be made to the decor of Springwood for the visit, which meant that the royal couple would be confronted in the entrance hall of the house with highly coloured prints depicting the defeat of British men-of-war by American forces in 1812. During the planning stages of the visit, Eleanor had raised the subject of the prints and the King's likely reaction to them. "My husband's reply was, 'I think he'll enjoy them!' And he did!" she revealed later.[13] As for the guest list for the dinner that the British embassy was planning to hold, the names had been chosen largely in accordance with protocol, but "the dinner will be none the less pleasant", Lindsay added, drily.

The following weekend, with just days to go, Eleanor went back to Hyde Park to prepare everything – sharing her hopes and concerns with readers of her column. On Monday, 5th June, she assured them that everything was ready. "I am glad to be able to say that, when I leave here Tuesday morning, I think all I can do for the comfort of our guests will have been done," she wrote. "Of course, an old house cannot be changed and my mother-in-law does not often entertain so many guests in her home, but she is enjoying her preparations very much. We hope everyone will be comfortable and happy."

Eleanor also reflected on what it must be like to be in the position of the King and Queen.

Sometimes I cannot help wondering whether royal visitors ever have the same kind of qualms about the people with whom they are going to stay, that we ordinary mortals have. I always wonder whether I shall have the right clothes and whether my hosts will find having people attached to the President's family more of a burden than a joy.

The young royalties, however, must realize by now how anxious everybody is to see them. The Queen has won the hearts of her Canadian subjects and many Americans by what they consider her courage and informality. The fact that she steps down into the crowds and that the King goes with her has, I think, made a tremendous impression. I don't doubt that those in charge of the safety of these two wish that they were easier to handle, but their actions are certainly making them very popular. This country as a whole feels great respect for the young King and Queen and everywhere you hear words of praise for the King's quiet and dignified bearing.

The next day, 6th June, after having had a long walk in the woods – which were still free of mosquitoes and flies – followed by her first swim of the year in the pool at Springwood, Eleanor wondered in her column whether the royal couple would want to follow suit. "I am sure they like to walk, for all the English people I have ever known enjoy that exercise and really know how to walk, not saunter," she said.

Eleanor was not so sure about swimming, though, especially since there had not been any reports of them taking to the water during the Canadian phase of the trip. "I rather hope that is because Canada is somewhat colder than the United States," she wrote. "The particular lakes where they have been resting must still be somewhat glacier-like. I remember swimming one summer in the St Lawrence River, when my husband was governor of New York and we were going from one canal to another along the river. It was very chilly amusement even in midsummer."

The next day, Eleanor was reflecting not only on all the gifts people were sending for the royals – which would have to be sent on to the embassy – but also about food that kept arriving that people hoped would be served. Others were writing in to express concern that a "hotel expert" was not being called in to order the food and oversee the cooking. "I hope that the food at the White House will be good," she wrote.

During the past six years the same people have struggled through the preparation of meals for visiting dignitaries and people of importance in our own country. I can only pray that serving a king and queen will not paralyze them! As the food at the big house in Hyde Park will be entirely in the hands of my mother-in-law, I know it will be good. My responsibility in Hyde Park is only for one picnic, and even if everything should go wrong, the only result would be to make our neighbours across the water realize that we are still a young country and don't do some things here as well as they do.

One of our neighbours used to say that the only advantage in not being too good a housekeeper is that your guests are so pleased to feel how very much better they are. I should not be at all surprised if some of the things which the King and Queen will remember and laugh over, when they return to their own fireside, will be the differences between the English way of doing things and the way they are done in Canada and in the United States.

Eleanor remained on the royal theme in the next day's column, expressing horror at reports of another royal drama from the other side of the Atlantic: a man with a sawn-off shotgun had fired three shots at the Duchess of Kent outside her home in Belgrave Square as she was on her way to the cinema in Haymarket in the West End of London. "How precariously royalty exists! How hard it must be to forget the constant anxiety of those about you!"

In the meantime, she continued to be bombarded with letters and comments about the royal visit from people she met. "There is no shadow of a doubt in my mind that there are few individuals in any walk of life who are not thinking and wondering about the King and Queen of England," she wrote. "If I needed any further proof, my mail would corroborate this. One of my most amusing letters tells me that on scanning over the menu for dinner at the White House, the writer finds that fish is to be served with a wine sauce, which should never be served with that kind of accompaniment. My correspondent may be soothed with the news that the fish course has been eliminated."

Chapter 11

Washington

Washington was ready to celebrate. At the Capitol, the Union Station and along Pennsylvania Avenue, some six hundred Union Jacks and Stars and Stripes were flown from trees and lamp posts. Arranged in groups of three, surmounting respectively the shields of Great Britain and the United States, the flags lined the route along which the royal couple would pass on their way to the White House. Along Connecticut Avenue and Dupont Circle, through which the couple were to travel to and from the British embassy, more flags and banners waved from the windows of shops and over the porticos of private houses.

Life, meanwhile, ground to a halt in anticipation of the visit: all government employees were to be free from 10 a.m. to 2 p.m., the large department stores were not to open until after noon and other businesses were to close from 11 a.m. to 12.30 p.m. The crowd was estimated at five hundred thousand. "Not since they burned the White House in 1814 have the British caused such a stir in the nation's capital as they are causing in connection with the visit of King George and Queen Elizabeth," commented one reporter.[1]

In the White House, Eleanor Roosevelt too was making last-minute preparations for the royal visit – which she continued to detail in her column. The evening before, three of her sons and their wives had arrived for dinner, but with the guest accommodation at the White House spoken for, they went to stay elsewhere – although Franklin Jr, their second-youngest, brought his Great Dane, which he left to stay at the White House until they all continued on to Hyde Park.

"I have just made the rounds of every room in the White House with Mrs Nesbitt, the housekeeper," Eleanor wrote on Thursday, 8th June, hours before the royal couple were due to arrive.

We even inspected the third floor, which, this time, instead of housing grandchildren, will have our royal visitors' personal servants. Ordinarily, when the house is going to be filled, I tell Mrs Nesbitt to get in touch with the nurses to find out what food should be ordered for the various children, but on this occasion I have no babies to worry about! I have to explain, however, with extreme care certain English customs, such as early-morning tea and bread and butter and water which must be cooled but must not have ice in it. Only in our own country is water with ice floating in it considered a necessity.

Reeves, the head gardener, meanwhile, had been working on the various floral displays, with the help of gifts received from around the country: a friend of Eleanor's in New Jersey sent roses, pink gladioli were dispatched from Alabama, while the orchids that were to be the centrepiece of the table for that evening's dinner came from another friend in New York City. The railings of the steps leading down to the garden were covered with honeysuckle in bloom, and the big magnolia tree planted by Andrew Jackson had opened wide its blossoms. "England is a land of beautiful gardens and flowers, but I do not think the magnolia will be duplicated there," she wrote.

Unlike her husband, who loved to put on a show, Eleanor admitted she had been dreading the prospect of all the pageantry. Yet even she was becoming more enthusiastic: "After all these preparations, it is exciting to reach the actual day of arrival and I am looking forward with keen pleasure to meeting two people who have impressed their sympathetic personalities upon a continent."

The Roosevelts, accompanied by other government officials, were at Union Station in the presidential reception room to greet the royal guests when their train arrived at eleven o'clock. The royal couple was escorted through the double line of marines by Cordell Hull, his wife and Ronald Lindsay.

Once the presentation was over, the President and his wife accompanied the King and Queen through the guard of honour, which was drawn up in front of the station. The band played the British national anthem and the

Star-Spangled Banner, and there was a twenty-one-gun salute. Then, after all the photographs were taken, the royal and the presidential couples climbed aboard their respective open cars and, with a military escort, set off at 11.45 a.m. along Delaware Avenue to the Capitol, and thence along Constitution Avenue to Pennsylvania Avenue, through Treasury Place and across East Executive Avenue to the south-east gate of the grounds of the White House.

The procession, which included detachments of cavalry and tanks, proceeded at walking pace; aircraft flew overhead. The sun was shining and the heat, way above ninety degrees Fahrenheit (more than thirty degrees Celsius), stifling. "Wearing Windsor uniform, gold braid with sun on it, in an open car, was almost like the top of a stove," noted Mackenzie King.[2] The King turned pale and was later to confide to Roosevelt that he had been worried several times during the journey that he might pass out.[3]

The crowds, both outside Union Station and lining the route, were massive, and their response extraordinarily enthusiastic. General Edwin "Pa" Watson, the President's senior military aide, told Lindsay he had seldom witnessed such a large turnout or seen visitors be given such a warm reception. Eleanor Roosevelt, meanwhile, was fascinated by the Queen's response. "She had the most gracious manner and bowed right and left with interest, actually looking at people in the crowd so that I am sure many of them felt that her bow was really for them personally," she recalled.[4] Despite the heat, a light cover had been placed by a footman over the Queen's knees when she got into the car; she and the King both sat on special cushions that Eleanor Roosevelt was amused to discover had springs in them to make all the waving easier.

Once inside the grounds of the White House, the royal couple entered the building through the south entrance. Immediately they arrived, what was known as a Diplomatic Circle was held for the heads of the diplomatic missions and their wives. When it was over, they went to rest for a few minutes before they assembled in the East Room. That afternoon, they drove into Washington, visiting the Lincoln Memorial, the Cathedral Church of St Peter and St Paul, Rock Creek Park and other places of interest. When they got back, the King and Queen changed and at 4.45 p.m. they left the White House through a line of Boy and Girl Scouts drawn up on South Executive Place for a garden party at the British embassy.

While the royal couple were out, Eleanor Roosevelt was amused to note that something of a rerun of the War of American Independence was being waged between the White House staff and those members of the royal entourage who were quartered in the servants' rooms. The host servants were initially fascinated by the visitors – "even in this country where people had shed their blood to be independent of a king, there is still an awe of and an interest in royalty and the panoply that surrounds it," as the First Lady put it.[5] Problems began, however, when Nesbitt complained that the King's valet was making what she considered unreasonable demands and daring to complain about the food and drink on offer.

The White House ushers were also struck by quite how caught up with protocol their British counterparts were. When one of them saw the Queen's maid walking through the second-floor hall she asked her if she would tell the lady-in-waiting that the Queen wanted her to come to her room. Drawing herself up to her full height, the maid declared "I am the Queen's maid" and swept off down the hall. The usher, exhausted with the extra work and the heat, resorted to some old-fashioned American slang, saying: "Oh, you're a big shot, hey?"

Eleanor Roosevelt also recounted an awkward incident when one of the messengers who fancied himself as an artist made a bad, almost life-size portrait of the Queen and asked one of the maids to leave it on her dressing table with a note requesting both her autograph and her opinion of it. When the Queen saw it, she had it removed. The artist was tracked down and given a telling off by an usher. "If that man ever again utters the word autograph, it will curdle in his throat," the usher said.

To call it the social event of the season would have been an understatement. The garden party held that afternoon in the grounds behind the British embassy, a recently built brick mansion two miles from the White House, had been the talk of the town – and a matter of some contention for those who thought they should have been included among the 1,350 invited guests but were inexplicably left out.

The bulk of the list was dictated by protocol: high-ranking administration officials, members of the diplomatic corps and senior members of the Congress and the Supreme Court had to receive their invitations. So, too, did leading members of the British community. It was over the few remaining places that the dispute was fiercest: Ambassador Lindsay and his wife, who were charged with drawing up the list, were accused of being snobs and blunderers by some of those excluded.

The *New York Times* captured the mood in an article on 21st May entitled 'A Tempest in a Teapot over Royal Garden Fete'. The ambassador, the newspaper claimed, had been "burdened with the toughest and most trivial task in his long and distinguished diplomatic service – the choice of 1,350 among many thousands who feel that when a king and queen have a party they should be there". The loudest protests, it claimed, came from newspaper managers annoyed that their special writers "who see a good piece behind the embassy garden wall are not on the list" and also from the wives of men "tufted with some prominence or another, who feel that to be left out of a group of 1,350 is a slight too public and too pointed to be borne".

"Do the American people as a whole care who is asked to the party and who isn't?" the newspaper concluded. "This correspondent does not think the American people care a hoot but may rather be noting with democratic regret that so many republican guests want to look closely at a queen." In the event, the guest list, which closed on 6th June, numbered 1,400 and, thanks to a few last-minute cancellations, managed to include all the members of the Senate and their wives.

Guests began pouring into the garden at the back of the embassy from about four o'clock under the watchful eye of plain-clothes detectives, who, according to one British observer, were all too conspicuous in their panama hats. The royal couple appeared on the portico at the rear at 4.40 p.m.: the King wearing a grey morning coat and top hat despite the heat, the Queen "looking for all the world like a Watteau painting, with her white lace picture gown, large white hat, long white gloves and ruffled organza parasol".[6] They were greeted by the ambassador and his wife, and then all four stood together as a British naval band struck up 'God Save the King'.

The royal couple were introduced to a select group of guests, among them Vice President John "Cactus Jack" Garner, known for his informal manner and wisecracks, who broke all rules of protocol by giving the King a big friendly slap on the back. And then the King and Queen separated and, accompanied by the ambassador and his wife respectively, made their way through the throng, stopping to talk to those who had been specially picked out for them. Among them were Admiral Richard E. Byrd, the Polar explorer, Hugh Wilson, who had served briefly as US ambassador to Berlin before being withdrawn the previous November, and J.P Morgan, the banker, with whom the King took tea. Then, as the skies darkened in anticipation of a threatened storm, the royal couple returned to the portico and made their farewells. The guests began to drift away, slowly at first, but then more quickly as streaks of lightning lit up the sky and torrents of rain began to stream down.

After the garden party the royal couple returned to the White House. To Eleanor's amazement, the Queen did not seem to have a hair out of place or a single crease in her dress. The First Lady could not understand how it was possible to remain so perfectly in character all the time, and her admiration for her guest only grew. That being said, she confided in Elliott that she found the Queen a "little self-consciously regal"[7] – but wisely kept that opinion out of her column.

That evening's dinner was a formal affair – though following American, rather than British, protocol: so the Queen, glittering in her diamonds, sat on the President's right, while the King was next to Eleanor. As for the food, it "lived down" to the usual appalling standards set by Nesbitt, who ran the White House household. Despite the importance of the occasion, Roosevelt, according to Elliott, had lacked "either time or inclination to prepare a formal speech".[8] When he stood – as ever, with the help of an aide, to toast the King, he did so on the basis of little more than a few scribbled notes that read: "Life of nation… Give thanks – bonds friendship. Greatest contrib., civiliz. example conduct relations. Because each lack fear – unfortif. neither aggress. No race episode… May understanding grow closer-friendship closer – Drink to health."

That unpromising raw material was transformed into the following, which was subsequently reproduced for the newspapers:

In the life of a nation, as in that of an individual, there are occasions that stand out in high relief. Such an occasion is the present one, when the entire United States is welcoming on its soil the King and Queen of Great Britain, of our neighbour Canada, and of all the far-flung British Commonwealth of Nations. It is an occasion for festivities, but it is also fitting that we give thanks for the bonds of friendship that link our two peoples.

I am persuaded that the greatest single contribution our two countries have been enabled to make to civilization, and to the welfare of peoples throughout the world, is the example we have jointly set by our manner of conducting relations between our two nations.

It is because each nation is lacking in fear of the other that we have unfortified borders between us. It is because neither of us fears aggression on the part of the other that we have entered no race of armaments, the one against the other.

The King and I are aware of a recent episode. Two small uninhabited islands in the centre of the Pacific became of sudden interest to the British Empire and to the United States as stepping stones for commercial airplanes between America and Australasia. Both nations claimed sovereignty. Both nations had good cases.

To have entered into a long-drawn-out argument could have meant ill will between us and delay in the use of the islands by either nation. It was suggested that the problem be solved by the joint use of both islands by both nations, and, by a gentleman's agreement, to defer the question of ultimate sovereignty until the year 1989. The passage of fifty years will solve many problems.

If this illustration of the use of methods of peace, divorced from aggression, could only be universally followed, relations between all countries would rest upon a sure foundation, and men and women everywhere could once more look upon a happy, prosperous and a peaceful world.

May this kind of understanding between our countries grow ever closer, and may our friendship prosper. Ladies and gentlemen, we drink to the health of His Majesty, King George VI.[9]

While the President's speech was largely impromptu, the King's response had been carefully scripted by Lindsay;

stripped of all "regal phrases" and polysyllables and expressed in the simplest of language, it was intended to express his own feelings and at the same time to "please the average friendly American to know what he feels". "The American people will always respect him as The King, but I want them also to acquire affection for him as the human being, just such an affection as they had for his father," the ambassador wrote in a note accompanying one of the drafts.[10]

At just over two hundred words, the speech was blissfully short: the King thanked his hosts for "the kind invitation" and "still kinder welcome", brought good wishes from Britain and Canada and ended: "And I pray that our two great nations may ever in the future walk together along the path of friendship in a world at peace."

Despite his stammer, the King managed to get through it well, scarcely without a hesitation. Mackenzie King was nevertheless struck, not for the last time during the trip, by how both King and President were linked by their respective disabilities. "I shall never forget that evening and seeing these two men, each of whom have achieved greatness through physical infirmity," he wrote. "The King having mastered himself completely by overcoming his stammering, and the President by overcoming infantile paralysis."[11]

It was a thought that appeared to have been shared by the Queen, who had had a pained expression as the President struggled to get up. Amid the formality, Garner continued to show his disdain for protocol by putting his arm around the King's back. In his diary, Harold Ickes, the US secretary of the interior, complained that the Vice President had "no breeding or natural dignity" and was treating the monarch as if he were his "poker crony".[12]

The dinner did not pass without incident, at least as far as the performers were concerned: Marian Anderson had been loath to sing Negro spirituals and only agreed to do so after she was persuaded that the royal party should be able to hear music that really was native to America. One of the folk singers, meanwhile, had been reported to the FBI as a communist likely to do something dangerous. After being frisked by both the American Secret Service men and those from Scotland Yard, he was apparently so frightened he could hardly sing. Watching the performance, Eleanor hoped that, despite the heat, he wouldn't reach for his handkerchief, since she was sure any sudden movement would cause members of both services to jump on him.

If the King had any doubts about the success of the visit, he needed to look no further than the newspapers, which the next day, 9th June, were almost universal in their praise of a couple described by the *New York Times* as "the living symbols of the world's greatest empire". For the *Washington Post*, the royal presence in the capital symbolized "the dawning of a new era in world history" in which Britain had come to accept that its former colony had "come of age and has great maturity before it". "The American people have now come to realize that they are inevitably a tremendous factor in the modern world," the newspaper commented. "With that realization comes a growing determination to have the United States play a truly constructive role in this difficult era." At the same time, the article stressed, the visit had helped to underline "how much British tradition means in a period when there is a serious threat to the ideals which the two countries hold in common".

For the popular papers, inevitably, it was more about the pair's personalities. "King George VI Captures Washington", screamed a headline in the tabloid *New York Daily Mirror*. George Dixon, a star writer for its rival the *New York Daily News*, who had followed the royal couple on the Canadian leg of their journey, declared: "There's no use in fighting any longer, folks. We may as well throw in the sponge and admit we're licked. Royalty throws us all."

As with other royal visits, both before and afterwards, however, it was the Queen who seemed to have made the biggest impression on a personal level. In a front-page story on 9th June headlined "Queen Captivates Capital Throngs", the normally staid *New York Times* heaped praise on Elizabeth. "The King's tour is the Queen's triumph," it declared, praising her dress sense, gardenia-white skin, unruffled nature and the charm with which she handled the crowds – and all despite temperatures "almost unendurable to natives of this city". The paper was also impressed by the way the King had "gratitude rather than pique for the skill and success with which England's Queen subtly attracts the spotlight which her diffident husband will not shun but does not relish". As one correspondent commented as the motorcade swept up Pennsylvania Avenue amid thunderous cheers: "That's the Queen. Give her a crowd and she mows 'em down."

The royal couple had no time to rest on their laurels; the second day of their visit to Washington brought another charged programme – and began with a surprise when the King made an unscheduled appearance at a press conference for the capital's "eighty leading women journalists", at which the Queen had been due to appear alongside Eleanor. Before the royal couple arrived, Eleanor had praised the Queen. "It is unusual to find in one so young and so compassionate an understanding of the conditions which push people to desperation," she told them. "Her Majesty seems to me to be particularly interested in social conditions and seems to have a keen sense of the difficulties under which many people live and work."[13]

At his own early-morning conference, meanwhile, the President was describing his royal visitors as "very, very delightful people". Just after ten o'clock, it was on to a reception at the British embassy for 1,500 members of the British colony, where the King was dressed in a morning coat and striped trousers. With the temperature already in the nineties, he did, however, allow himself to go without the silk hat normally worn with them.

Next was probably the most important event of the day: a visit to Congress. Although the King had successfully resisted the suggestion that he make a formal address, a reception was held to allow him to meet its members in the rotunda. Before sunrise crowds had begun to gather along the route the pair would take; they burst into spontaneous applause as they caught sight of the car with the royal couple, which was escorted by motorcycle police and followed by another carload of Secret Service men.

Some ten thousand of the lucky ones, mostly wives of cabinet officers, high government officials and newspaper correspondents, were seated in camp chairs on a reserved space in front of the East Portico, where American presidents traditionally take their oath of office. Rather than drive straight past, though, the King and Queen got out and spent a few minutes strolling up and down so that everyone in the camp chairs could get a good view of them.

By then running five minutes late, the royal couple were met at the entrance by a silk-hatted delegation dressed in morning coats, led by Senator Key Pittman, chairman of the Committee on Foreign Relations. They made their way into the building, preceded by two sergeants-at-arms, who led the way with bowed heads and hats in hand.

The mood among the congressmen waiting behind a velvet rope was a mixed one; many seemed nervous and self-conscious at the prospect of meeting royalty. A reporter from the *New York Times* described the atmosphere: "The House members were cutting up and making raucous noises, but as the funereal vanguard of the King and Queen appeared there were reproving 'sh's' from the more dignified Senate group, nearly all of whom are older than the British sovereigns."[14] Silence followed, although when the Queen appeared reporters heard murmurs of "She's lovely" and "She's just as sweet as she can be" coming from the ranks of the senators.

The chamber was full of reminders of the two countries' complicated past relations. The King and Queen stood on a strip of blue carpet next to a life-size statue of Thomas Jefferson holding in his hand the Declaration of Independence and two statues of George Washington. Facing them across the rotunda was a huge painting of the surrender of the redcoat army of Lord Cornwallis at Yorktown in 1781 that ended the last major land battle of the War of Independence. One by one, seventy-four senators and then 357 of the 435 members of the House filed past, shaking the King's hand. They were led by William Borah, the isolationist senator from Idaho, dressed up for the occasion in a morning suit that he told friends had "been in mothballs for thirty-five years".[15]

"Cousin George, I bring you greetin's from the far-flung regions of the Empire State of Texas," said Representative Net Patton, shaking the King's hand.[16] Turning to the Queen, he said: "How do you do, Cousin Elizabeth? Why, you are much prettier than your picture. You are almost as pretty as the girls of Texas."

"What a charming thing to say," the Queen replied.[17]

Another representative, Robert Mouton of Louisiana, addressed the couple in French and kissed the Queen's hand – getting a warm smile in response.

The King gave as good as he got, however, greeting Senator Ellison D. Smith of South Carolina, whom he had met at the garden party the previous day, by his nickname "Cotton Ed". He also gave Senator Key Pittman a taste of his dry humour.

"You have some beautiful pictures," the King said, surveying canvases depicting early American history.

"Yes," replied Pittman. "Here, for instance, Your Majesty, is one depicting the baptism of Pocahontas."

At that point, the King's eye surveyed other paintings, including the one of Cornwallis, and he added, with a twinkle in his eye: "I see you have some pictures of a later period, too."[18]

The King managed to shake hands with all 431 present in twenty-five minutes flat. Later they broke up into small groups, and the King was seen walking arm-in-arm with Senator Sol Bloom and exchanging jokes with Vice President Garner.

As the royal couple turned to go, those present broke into applause. "Her Majesty and I are unable to express our appreciation of the universal courtesy and friendship we have received," the King told Pittman. It was mutual: Patton had been especially taken by the Queen. "If America can keep Queen Elizabeth, Congress will regard Britain's war debt as settled," he quipped later. As Gordon put it: "It was with mutual regret that the function, which had begun in a serious fashion and had ended like party of old friends, came to a conclusion."[19]

Time was pressing, however. From Congress, the King and Queen drove to the presidential yacht, the USS *Potomac*, where Roosevelt and his wife were waiting for them.

"Well, how did you make out?" the President was heard asking after a twenty-one-gun salute announced their arrival.

With the Royal Standard and the President's personal flag flying fore and aft, they sailed down the Potomac, past wooded shores, to Washington's tomb. There, like his grandfather and brother before him, the King laid a wreath of lilies and irises, tied with a ribbon of the royal colours of red, white and blue, on a plain sarcophagus marked "Washington". Such a tribute – this time from a reigning British monarch – to the man who had wrested independence from George III seemed to commemorate the fact that, once and for all, differences of opinion between the United Kingdom and America had been settled. It was then on to Arlington National Cemetery, where the King laid wreaths at the Tomb of the Unknown Soldier and the Canadian Cross of Sacrifice in commemoration of the first war in which the United States and the British Empire had made common cause.

That evening the two couples, Mackenzie King and various other dignitaries dined informally at the British embassy, and then it was off to Union Station, where the *Royal Blue* train was waiting to take them on to Red Bank, New Jersey, and their next day in New York. Although it was nearly midnight, the station was teeming with press photographers and sightseers keen to catch a glimpse of the couple. With a hiss of steam and a piercing whistle that cut through the roar of the crowd, the train edged out of the station. At last, the royal couple had a few hours of peace.

Chapter 12

New York

"He's Here", screamed the headline of the *New York Post* in letters an inch and a half high. "Millions of New Yorkers Roar Welcome to British Sovereigns," said the *New York Sun*. "Our nation today welcomes King George and Queen Elizabeth," declared the *New York World Telegram*. "They are greeted by the American people not merely as representatives of another great democracy, or as royalty, but as two great human beings who have won that distinction in their own right […] We like them. And we hope they like us."[1]

Shortly before nine o'clock, crowds were already packed around the station of Redbank, New Jersey, which had been elaborately decorated for the arrival of the royal couple. People glanced excitedly along the tracks, shimmering in the light of the morning sun, for a first glimpse of the train. Then a plume of smoke appeared round the corner, and a moment later the locomotive slid into sight. Stepping down from the carriage, the Queen, dressed in a blue-crêpe ensemble with matching hat and a parasol, "looked particularly fresh and radiant, almost as if she were coming from a vacation in the country", wrote one contemporary observer.[2] At her side was the King, wearing grey morning clothes and a grey top hat. They were greeted by Arthur Harry Moore, the governor of New Jersey, and his wife.

As the King stood to attention, the band played 'God Save the King'. After it finished, he remained in the same position for a few seconds, expecting the Star-Spangled Banner. It never came. The day's events were intended as a celebration of Britishness. The press were again out in force: to the amusement of the royal couple, the photographers kept up a running commentary as they snapped away. "Come on, now let's get the Queen's smile," shouted one. It was very different from the kind of reception they were used to at home. As ten US Air Force planes flew back and forth, the royal couple made their way to the big open car that was to carry them to Fort Hancock. The short route was lined with cheering crowds, held back by State Troopers in their blue uniforms, armed with fully loaded rifles and bayonets. The authorities were taking no chances.

They travelled on past the green fields and luxuriant trees of the New Jersey countryside. Crowds waving Union Jacks lined the streets and sat in the gnarled old elms to get a better view. Young girls scattered flowers from baskets in front of the advancing cars. The whole population of the state seemed to have turned out. The Queen appeared close to tears as they passed a county hospital and patients, some of them in wheelchairs, waved their greetings. Every fifty yards stood a soldier with rifle loaded and bayonet fixed. As they

PETER CONRADI

neared the coast, the trees and fields gave way to buildings and wider roads. The beach was already full of bathers, who came towards the road as they heard the royal motorcade. And then there were cries of "Glad to see you King!" and "Happy to have you both with us", which prompted smiles from the royal couple, the Queen waving back demurely and the King raising his hat. Everyone seemed in a holiday mood.

The US destroyer *Warrington* was waiting to take them on to the next stage of their journey, its grey hull and brass work gleaming in the sunshine, and the Royal Standard flying from its mast. Their destination was the Battery on the southern tip of Manhattan Island, the gateway to New York City. First, though, there was yet another rendition of God Save the King. As the King and Queen walked on board the vessel, pipes shrilled and the sailors clad in white who lined the rails came stiffly to attention. A royal salute of guns boomed from a neighbouring cruiser and the Royal Standard broke from the yardarm of the *Warrington* – the first time since the founding of the United States that any of its ships had flown the flag of its former ruler. This was a signal for pandemonium to break out across the harbour as liners, ferryboats, tugs and steamers all sounded their sirens, while the band on the shore continued to play.

As the royal couple stood on the bridge, acknowledging the roar of the crowd, the *Warrington* set off across the sunlit waters of the Hudson. Ahead of it steamed minesweepers that cleared a path; astern and on either side came an escort of thirty coastguard vessels that fanned out across the wide stretch of water. Then came a fleet of ferryboats, many of them chartered by New York's British residents, and all packed with cheering spectators; from their decks balloons emblazoned with Union Jacks were released into the sky.

Sitting on deck, the King and Queen gazed for the first time at the New York skyline, which had been transformed by the frenzy of skyscraper construction of the 1920s and 1930s. Every now and then they would point to a famous landmark: the Chrysler Building, the tallest in the world when it was completed in 1930, and the Empire State Building, which stole its crown when it was finished just eleven months later. When the Statue of Liberty loomed into the view through the mist, they sprang up out of their deckchairs to take in the spectacle.

As they neared the coast, the royal couple could have been excused a sense of awe: the whole of New York seemed to have come out to greet them. Stretching from the quayside to the entrance to the World's Fair were some four million people. The destroyer's approach served as a signal for a dozen bands to start playing 'God Save the King', all at a slightly different tempo and with slight variations. The crowds cheered, planes circled overhead and the fireboats sent great plumes of water into the air. Appearing at the head of the gangplank, the King and Queen stood almost frozen for a moment and contemplated what lay in front of them.

"It was a scene that one could hardly believe even when witnessing it," wrote one observer.

As the first cheers from the water's edge rolled along the causeway, the vast crowd took it up until the roaring welcome became a colossal volume of sound, punctuated at intervals by the thundering of the guns at Fort Jay where the royal salute was being fired. Blaring motor-car horns, rattles, factory hooters, bugles – all added to the din. Although it was only 11.15 a.m., the whole town had taken the day off to witness a spectacle which they would never see again, and which will be remembered as one of the most sensational days in the whole long history of the United States.[3]

The welcoming delegation stood on a red carpet three hundred foot long, from which a few minutes earlier a tabby cat, licking itself clean in a leisurely way in front of one hundred thousand people, had been chased away by a horrified janitor. First to greet the King was Herbert Lehman, the bald-headed governor of New York State and son of the founder of the bank that bore his name. He was followed by Fiorello LaGuardia, the squat but energetic mayor of the city. "All New Yorkers are in love with you already," LaGuardia told the Queen – out of reach of the microphone.[4]

It took just two minutes for Lehman and LaGuardia to pronounce the words of greeting, but the fourteen thousand policemen struggled to hold back the swaying crowd, so much so that one of the officers was inadvertently pushed into the water, with a loud splash, much to the amusement of the spectators. Then they all walked to an open car that was to carry them at the head of a procession of thirteen gleaming black vehicles, surrounded by police on motorcycles, on an eight-mile journey through the city to the World's Fair. The Queen got in first, sitting down on the left, but then the King stooped and whispered to her. Convinced that she was the one the spectators really wanted to see, and realizing that most of them were standing to the right of their path, he urged her to change sides. His gesture earned a roar of approval from the crowd.

There was a moment of humour, too, when a mounted policeman galloped down the road ahead of the convoy, prompting a wag in the crowd to yell: "What's the matter?" The quick-witted policeman turned in his saddle and shouted "The British are coming", in an echo of the cry of Paul Revere, one of the heroes of the War of Independence, who had warned of the British advance on Boston.

During the journey, the King had a further opportunity to endear himself to the crowd. It had been decided that the convoy would travel at a steady fifty miles an hour along the express highway, but he realized this meant he and the Queen were little more than a blur to those standing beside the road. Leaning over the side of the open car, he beckoned to one of the policemen riding alongside. "Will you find someone in charge and ask him if it will be possible for us to slow down," he asked. "It is impossible for us to see the crowds, and I am sure they can't see this."[5]

The message was passed through, thanks to one of the most elaborate two-way radio hook-ups ever used in the city, which allowed the police department to keep a minute-by-minute record of the royal party's progress. And so they halved the speed of the convoy to twenty-five miles an hour. It completely threw out the day's tightly packed schedule, but gained the King the appreciation of the crowd.

Then, as the convoy turned into West Street, the royal couple had a first taste of a typical New York greeting. When the trip was being planned, there had been discussion about their precise route through the city and whether they should be accorded that most characteristic of welcomes: a ticker-tape parade along Broadway. LaGuardia was a strong advocate, but Roosevelt warned the British side against contemplating a ride through New York's packed streets, largely out of concern at the difficulty of controlling the crowds. This did not prevent the spectators from improvising one of their own: despite explicit orders that no ticker tape or pieces of torn-up telephone books should be thrown out of the windows, people living along the route did just that, sending a storm of paper and streamers floating down onto the motorcade.

It remained a matter of regret to LaGuardia – and also to his guests – that they had not chosen a route that would have taken them along Broadway. "I don't know whether it is just my own disappointment about not being able to take them up Fifth Avenue and Broadway, but I gathered that they would have preferred that route," he told journalists afterwards. "As we drove up the West Side Highway both the King and Queen asked several times how far we were from Broadway, and how far from Fifth Avenue."[6]

And then it was on through Central Park, which was packed with thousands of spectators, many of whom had camped out all night to get a good view, and along Seventy-Second Street. At Triborough Bridge, which spans the East River, the crowd broke through the police cordon and a group of women somehow got hold of the Queen's bouquet, which they fell upon, ripping off the flowers and ribbons as souvenirs. Order was finally restored, and the convoy continued to Flushing Meadow and the World's Fair.

Formally opened on 30th April 1939 on the site of what had previously been a notorious garbage dump in Queens, the New York World's Fair was the biggest international event since the end of the First World War. More than two hundred thousand people turned out for the opening day; by the time it closed in October 1940, a total of forty-four million had passed through its doors.

The event had been conceived four years earlier, at the height of the Great Depression, by a group of retired New York policemen as a way of boosting the economy both of the city and of the country as a whole. They then formed the New York World's Fair Corporation, which from its offices near the top of the Empire State Building set out to turn their idea into reality. The Fair, which drew exhibitors from across the world, allowed visitors to take a look at "the world of tomorrow" and had as its opening slogan "Dawn of a New Day". Although some such as Albert Einstein saw the event as a chance to showcase science, Grover Whalen, the former chief of police who became president of its committee, saw it in commercial terms as an opportunity for corporations to present their products to consumers.

One of the main attractions was Futurama, sponsored by General Motors: over a space of 36,000 square feet, visitors were transported over a huge diorama of the United States, complete with miniature towns, highways, fifty thousand vehicles and five hundred thousand homes. In rival Chrysler's exhibit, visitors could see a Plymouth car being assembled before their eyes. Among the pioneering products on show were television sets, colour photography, nylon, air conditioning, fluorescent lamps and "Smell-O-Vision", a system to release odours into cinema during films – which, decades later, was voted by readers of *Time* magazine one of the hundred worst ideas of the twentieth century.

The Fair's overtly commercial rationale had initially prompted questions in London as to whether it would be appropriate for the King to attend.[7] Its symbols, the two modernist structures known as the Trylon and Perisphere, seemed to appear in every advertisement and souvenir shop in America. Might there not be the danger that this would be seen as some kind of royal commercial endorsement? Another thought was to have the complex closed to ordinary visitors for the day. In the end, the event's "world of tomorrow" theme seemed irresistible, not least as the British pavilion was one of the largest in the international zone.

The organizers were delighted at the boost the royal visit would bring, even if the preparations required were massive: in late April, Canning of the Yard had toured the route that the King and Queen would follow within the fairgrounds as a safety precaution. Then, the day before the royal visit, Whalen, accompanied by Captain Leary of the United States Navy and Lieutenant Colonel Parker of the United States Army, made the same journey, often bending down on their hands and knees to examine the paving to ensure it was smooth enough. Whalen commented that building the "world of tomorrow" was not half the job of smoothing the bumps for the King and Queen.

The royal motorcade approached the Fair along newly built Grand Central Parkway, and at 12.38 p.m., half an hour behind schedule, they entered through the Fair's Boulevard Gate. A twenty-one-gun salute rang out, shattering a glass case in nearby Washington Hall that contained George Washington's signet ring. More than one hundred thousand visitors – one of the highest ever on a single day – had begun to pour into the grounds when the gates opened at nine o'clock. Each received a souvenir card certifying that

PETER CONRADI

they had been there on the day of the royal visit. Between the Lagoon of Nations and the Court of Peace were two gigantic portraits of the King and Queen: measuring twelve by eighteen foot, they were mounted in elaborate gilt frames twenty by thirty foot and placed on pedestals five foot high. The originals were enlarged four hundred times thanks to a process originated by Eastman Kodak.

Some 3,376 uniformed policemen and four to five hundred additional security men kept the public back twenty feet from the couple; many took to the roofs of the pavilion to get a better view. All sweltered in the heat, which by noon had reached eight-three degrees. Security remained high: every thirty minutes, Secret Service men searched every telephone booth in the grounds to guard against possible bomb plots.

Whalen, whose presidency of the Fair had earned him a place on the cover of *Time* magazine that May, greeted and escorted the King and Queen to the private elevator. As they ascended, the King turned to him and asked: "When do we eat?" The answer was only after a long and grandiose welcoming ceremony. And so the royal couple were led into the main reception room, decorated with £137,000-worth of antiques for the occasion. As they entered, they walked over a carpet that had once belonged to Louis XIV; on the reception dais they stood on a brilliant yellow rug that had been made for a shah of Persia in the seventeenth century. White peonies stood in jars of exquisite Chinese porcelain, and a Gobelin tapestry hung on one of the walls.

After the royal couple had been presented with versions of the Trylon and Perisphere in gold and crystal, they got down to the arduous task in hand: greeting hundreds of official city and state administrators and members of New York's social elite. Divided into groups of ten, the chosen few – who amounted to 560 – were escorted to the royal couple by girl marshals in blue uniforms and round, flat straw hats. They first bowed or curtsied, but sensing their discomfort, the Queen suggested they shake hands instead. Italy's Commissioner General Giuseppe Cantù refused and raised his arm in a Fascist salute, sending a murmur through the crowd. The Queen, though usually unflappable, looked totally taken aback for a moment.

The King managed to get through about half the line, but there was still a long stretch of dignitaries in front of him, and he and the British party were beginning to lose their cool. It had been agreed that Whalen would present just sixty people: now the King was expected to greet almost ten times as many. There then ensued what Lindsay described, with typical diplomatic understatement, as a "slight hitch in proceedings". With his hand beginning to hurt – and feeling even hungrier – the King walked over to Mackenzie King and told him he could not possibly shake hands with everyone else. This was communicated to Whalen, and the royal pair went to leave – to the dismay of those still waiting, among them Mrs Vincent Astor, glamorous in a purple-and-black print gown, and Edward Roosevelt, a cousin of the First Lady, who actually worked at the Fair.

"What the hell are you doing?" Mayor LaGuardia demanded of Whalen.

"Don't ask me, Fiorello, ask him," the Fair's president said as he rushed off after the royal party.

Finally, it was time for lunch for eighty-two in the Federal Building. Preparations had been extensive: the Queen's powder room had been designed in shades of pink and dove-grey, with a theme of tropical birds and luxuriant foliage. The Secret Service had swept the entire place the day before, and guards had prevented anyone else getting in since.

As the couple entered the yellow-and-grey dining room, the Queen was greeted by Meyer Davis's orchestra with the tune 'Beautiful Lady'. The great maple-wood dining table was decorated with crystal bowls holding hundreds of red and white roses. The gold plates carried the American coat of arms and stars representing the forty-eight states of the Union. The usual staff had been replaced with a specially selected corps of twenty waiters, who wore formal evening dress and white ties and white gloves; the six wine-bearers were in greyish-blue uniforms. Cocktails were served a few minutes before they all sat down: the King took one, though the Queen declined hers. The menu was all-American and started with "New England Sea Food Cocktail" and "Jellied Gumbo Louisiana"; it continued with "Breast of Capon – Maryland Style",

"Corn Fritters", "Alligator Pear and Grapefruit Salad" and "Washington Log".

While the royal party feasted in formal splendour, there was a touch of spontaneity outside: the New York Fire and Police Department began to play popular melodies, and the Boy and Girl Scouts, who were waiting to greet the royal couple, passed the time dancing. As the music and sounds of laughter filtered into the dining room, Mayor LaGuardia went to the window and was greeted by cheers: they grew louder as first the Queen and then the King waved.

Lunch over, the pair set off to visit the various exhibits aboard a "jitterbug", a special trackless train decorated with American and British flags, with the King at the wheel driving at two miles an hour rather than the twenty of which it was capable. They took in the various British Empire exhibits, culminating in the British Pavilion, where they were met by the usual barrage of introductions and hands to shake. Then, walking up the Pavilion's steps, guarded by two huge stylized lions modelled on those that decorated London's flagpoles during his coronation, the King toured the exhibits, stopping for the longest at the case displaying a copy of the Magna Carta, which had been lent by Lincoln Cathedral. The Queen, meanwhile, took special interest in an exhibition of Scottish industry. "It's still the 10th of June, isn't it? We've been up so long I feel it must be another day," quipped the King, as the strain began to show.

Once they had completed the visit, and by now running almost an hour late, he and the Queen left by one of the secondary exits. Then it was on to their next engagement: a short visit to Columbia University. After driving past crowds of cheering students gathered on the campus, they escaped the heat and walked into the cool of the university's Memorial Library. There, after a brief address by its president, Dr Nicholas Murray Butler, the King and Queen wrote their names in the register and inspected the charter that had been granted to the university by King George II.

That evening, exhausted, they drove the eighty miles or so from New York out through the Hudson Valley. The whole of the road had been closed to traffic, allowing the sixteen limousines carrying the royal party and their twelve-strong motorcycle escort to move at fifty miles an hour or more. Spectators, some of whom had waited for several hours, formed an unbroken line for the first twenty miles, waving British and American flags. In Poughkeepsie, some two hundred thousand people turned out, kept in place by ropes, police and troops. The route was so well guarded that the President's son, James, had difficulty getting through the police lines when he set off about an hour ahead of the royal motorcade in his battered old car.

The royal visit to the Fair, the American press almost unanimously agreed, had been an undoubted success. "On Flushing Meadows, where the redcoats of George III fought the ragged Continentals a century and a half ago, King George VI reigned for an afternoon," declared the *New York Times*.[8]

Chapter 13

Hot Dogs and Cocktails

It was not until 8 p.m. that the King and Queen finally arrived at Springwood. "The programme of the Royal Tour had got somewhat out of hand," was how the King's official biographer put it.[1] As the car stopped in front of the house, Roosevelt, his wife and his mother came out onto the porch to receive their guests. The greetings over, the royal couple went to their rooms, changed and appeared in the library. The King walked towards Roosevelt and the table with the cocktails he had prepared earlier.

"My mother does not approve of cocktails and thinks you should have a cup of tea," Roosevelt told him.

"Neither does my mother," the King replied, taking a cocktail.[2]

They sat down to eat at 9.30 p.m., an hour and a half behind schedule. There were thirty of them around the table, including many members of the Roosevelt family. The President and his royal guests quickly hit it off. The King, as Roosevelt later confided to Daisy, was "grand, with an almost American sense of humour – he never seemed to miss the funny side of anything [...] showed an extraordinary

knowledge of this country, the people, and important individuals and always said something appropriate on meeting
them – He was completely natural and put all the 'royalness'
aside when in private."[3] Mackenzie King also noted the
relaxed atmosphere: "Most enjoyable […] a sort of family
affair", the Canadian Prime Minister wrote in his diary.[4]

Roosevelt even tried out some of his oldest and not very
funny jokes on his guests to test their sense of humour. "The
King rocked back & forward with laughter, repeating over
& over, 'It can't be true – it can't be true,'" the President
told Daisy. His wife was another matter: "The Queen, on the
other hand, could *never* quite forget that she was a queen &
is a little lacking in humour, though a fine person. Both are
extraordinarily kind & considerate of everyone."[5]

That didn't stop Roosevelt from proposing a toast to
the Queen, something never done in Britain, which left
Ambassador Lindsay open-mouthed. The Queen was
taken aback, but she joined in and drank to her own good
health. There was more drama to come: just a week earlier,
Roosevelt had received from the city of Limoges a beautiful
120-piece set of china, which was now being used for the
dinner. While they were eating, a little old serving table with
twenty-four of the plates standing on it collapsed without
warning, sending the crockery crashing to the floor. Sara
Roosevelt tried to ignore the incident and pretend nothing
had happened, but her stepdaughter-in-law, Mrs James
Roosevelt Roosevelt, from whom she had borrowed some

plates for the evening, could be heard saying: "I hope none of my dishes were among those broken."[6]

The matter of who was going to serve the guests at Hyde Park had been a subject of contention. The Roosevelts had brought their black butler with them from the White House – much to the consternation of Sara's English butler, who was normally in charge at Springwood. He was so appalled at the thought of the King and Queen being served by a black man that he took his holiday before the visit in order not to witness what he considered a slight to his country's royal family.

This White House butler was responsible for the second disaster of the evening. The President and his guests went down to the library after dinner and, just after they had settled down, there was a terrible crash: the butler, who was carrying a tray with bottles of ginger ale, decanters and glasses, tripped on the two steps leading down from the hall and slipped straight into the library. The contents of the tray were scattered over the floor, leaving a large pool of water and ice cubes. Eleanor found the whole thing amusing and, to the horror of her mother-in-law, wrote about it in her newspaper column.

The King, too, saw the funny side. "That's number two, what will be the next?" he asked.[7] (He wouldn't have to wait long: the next morning when the butler appeared for breakfast with a large tray laden with freshly cooked eggs and toast, he bumped into the mantelpiece and dropped it all on the floor.)

After dinner the women retired, while the King, Roosevelt and Mackenzie King withdrew to the library to discuss matters of state. The prospect of talking politics with the President of the United States must have been a daunting one for a monarch whose role was largely apolitical. He was well briefed however: thanks to the "Vade Mecum" written by Lindsay, which ran to dozens of pages and was divided into two sections: domestic politics, with chapters on subjects such as "History of Individualism", "New Deal and Its Achievements" and "Supreme Court Question", and foreign affairs, touching on "War debts", "Neutrality and Neutrality Laws" and "The European Crisis". It also contained a "good thumbnail sketch of the defects in the President's character which have been responsible for impeding him in achieving his full aims".[8] Thoroughly briefed, the King appears to have acquitted himself well.

Inevitably the main subject was impending war with Germany. Much of the conversation was taken up by the relationship between the United States and Canada – which, according to Roosevelt, was so close it would have been a "waste of money" to build a Canadian fleet, since he had already laid his plans to defend his neighbour's Pacific coast. Britain's position was more difficult: as Roosevelt told the King, he was deeply sympathetic to his country's plight, but pointed out how his hands were tied by the Neutrality Act, which was intended to keep America from being entangled in foreign wars. "His whole conversation with the King was to the effect that every possible assistance short of actual participation in war could be given," Mackenzie King noted in his diary. "He added that he hoped he might get freed of the Neutrality Act. Was not sure how long Congress might continue to delay its consideration [...]. He was going to try, however, to see if he could not get it repealed."[9]

That being said, the King, in his own account of their talk, was pleased to note that the President "gave us hope that something could be done to make it less difficult for the USA to help us". Roosevelt described how he and Cordell Hull were working to try to change isolationist attitudes, especially in the rural Midwest, where they were strongest, by pointing out to farmers there how much they would suffer in the case of a German victory. "How would you like to lose one of your best customers, the United Kingdom?" the President said he had told them.[10]

During their far-reaching conversation, the King also claimed the Germans had been spying on Britain for years and said he suspected his German relatives of acting as a conduit for sensitive information. His late father, George V, he said, had vowed never to shake hands with the German ambassador again. "I could see that the King felt very strongly about the whole way Germany had acted," noted Mackenzie King. "There was a family feeling as well as a national feeling."[11] For obvious reasons, the King did not bring up the matter of his own elder brother and his meeting with Hitler.

According to Mackenzie King's account, the King then spoke "very intimately" about Winston Churchill, at that time in the political wilderness, describing how he held him responsible for the disastrous Gallipoli campaign during the First World War. "The King indicated he would never wish to appoint Churchill to any office unless it was absolutely necessary in time of war," Mackenzie King wrote. "I confess I was glad to hear him say that because I think Churchill is one of the most dangerous men I have ever known."[12]

By about 1.30 a.m., the President, casting himself in a fatherly role towards the monarch, who was thirteen years his junior, tapped him gently on the knee and said, "Young man, it's time for you to go to bed." Far from being offended by such informality, the King seemed to enjoy it. He had been delighted by the frankness of the conversation, the first proper one he had ever had with a world leader. "Why don't my ministers talk to me as the President did tonight?" he asked Mackenzie King. "I felt exactly as though a father were giving me his most careful and wise advice."[13] Roosevelt was equally impressed. Jotting down his impressions of his guests, he wrote: "They are very delightful and understanding people, and, incidentally, know a great deal not only about foreign affairs in general but also about social legislation."[14] Lindsay's briefing notes had clearly served their purpose.

Before turning in for the night, the King invited Mackenzie King to join him in his room to reflect on their conversation with Roosevelt. Speaking of the trip, the Canadian told the King "that doing so much in so short a time might be very trying on the Queen and himself, but that [...] it was helping to save the world". From the King's response, Mackenzie King could see "that he was tremendously pleased that they had been personally able to play a very real part, and standing on their two feet, and getting recognition on account of themselves in a foreign country, not merely from their subjects".[15]

Sunday morning meant church. It had been announced that the royal couple would attend Divine Worship with the Roosevelts at the little church of St James, Hyde Park, where generations of the presidential family had worshipped. It only had room for two hundred people, and Reverend Frank Wilson had been so overwhelmed with requests for seats that he had had his telephone cut off a week earlier. He decided to allocate places according to who had attended most regularly over the previous twelve months. Long before dawn, people started to gather outside the building, determined to occupy the points that offered the best view of the royal visitors. Hawkers selling British and American flags began to ply their trade.

Daisy Suckley woke early. "June 11 was a red letter day," she wrote in her diary. She left home in a car provided by John Newman, the family's former chauffeur, and, armed with her admission card and special parking permit, set off towards the church. "I was so early that the police knew nothing about it & [I] drove all the way to the village & back." By then it was ten o'clock, but the doors to the church were not due to open for another hour, so, while she waited, the vicar's wife, "shaking with excitement", introduced her to some of the locals.[16]

Once inside, Daisy was pleased to see she had been given a good seat, second from the aisle, and for an hour enjoyed hearing the locals comment on the important people as they came in. When Helen Astor arrived, the girl on Daisy's right, getting over her shyness, turned to her and whispered:

"Do you know who that is? It's Mrs Vincent Astor."

"Oh-ooo-ooo," replied Daisy.

The numbers outside had grown to about fifty thousand by the time the royal party arrived on the dot of 11 a.m. The King, wearing a blue-grey lounge suit and without a hat, had travelled in one car with Roosevelt, who was dressed in white. The Queen, wearing mauve, came with Eleanor and the President's mother in another car.

The four front pews on the left-hand side facing the altar had been reserved for the presidential party. Sara and the Queen walked up together, followed by the King, who escorted Eleanor. The President came next, leaning heavily on his eldest son Jimmy's arm, with Tommy Qualters, his Secret Service agent and "walking partner", at his elbow. Suckley noted that Roosevelt was walking with great difficulty. "He told me later that only one side of his right brace was fastened & if it had broken, he would have collapsed in the aisle," she wrote. The church was so full that when one worshipper arrived, wearing flannel trousers and a short-sleeved tennis shirt, he was ushered into a pew with the royal party.

Before passing over to the visiting Episcopalian bishop Henry St George Tucker, Wilson briefly addressed his congregation, swollen way beyond normal numbers. "On behalf of the parish, I would like to extend a cordial welcome to Their Majesties, who are the President's guests," he said. "Looking round the church today, I would like to commend other members of the congregation to do likewise, and bring their guests in future."[17]

The Queen was struck by how familiar it all sounded – even if they were more than three thousand miles from home. "The service is exactly the same as ours down to every word, & they even had the prayers for the King and the Royal Family," she wrote to her mother-in-law. "I could not help thinking how curious it sounded, & yet how natural. It was just the sort of situation you would have appreciated – the drama of this happening in these days."[18] At the end of the service, a customary prayer was said for the President, followed by one for the royal couple, Queen Mary and the two princesses – the only change being the substitution of "the" for "our". The choir filed out to Kipling's 'Recessional'. The only question mark was over Tucker's sermon, partly on the subject of social reform, which Mackenzie King thought rather "too much of an essay and too long" – an opinion shared by both King and President, who considered it "a bit off the mark, having regard to the occasion".[19]

After posing for a photograph outside the church, the royal couple returned to the President's house and changed into cooler clothes – the King into a grey flannel suit and the Queen into a white dress. Then it was time for the picnic – which was to be held about three miles away at Dutchess Hill Cottage. The President drove them there in his Ford; the Queen found it a terrifying experience. "Motorcycle police cleared the road ahead of us," she recalled, "but the President pointed out the sights, waved his cigarette holder about, turned the wheel and operated the accelerator and the brake all with his hands. He was conversing more than watching the road and drove at great speed. There were several times when I thought we could go right off the road and tumble down the hills. It was a relief to get to the picnic."[20]

Eleanor, who had travelled ahead, was already there to welcome the guests. The most important ones were placed at seven tables on the porch, while about a hundred others, including the farm servants, gardeners and other domestic staff from Hyde Park, sat on chairs on the lawn. "It was a very friendly affair, and quite cool & pleasant," the Queen wrote to her mother-in-law.[21]

MENU FOR PICNIC AT HYDE PARK
Sunday, June 11, 1939

Virginia Ham

Hot Dogs (if weather permits)

Smoked Turkey

Cranberry Jelly

Green Salad

Rolls

Strawberry Shortcake

Coffee, Beer, Soft Drinks

The meal, served in informal style on paper plates, was classic picnic fare. But what of that most controversial and talked-about item on the menu? Eleanor had made clear beforehand that hot dogs would not be served if the weather were too hot, since they would need to be cooked on a brazier. But although it was almost eighty-five degrees in the shade, the King and Queen were so insistent on trying this strange delicacy that Eleanor ordered that the brazier should nevertheless be lit. The honours were done by Colonel Henry Ostaghen, from the US Treasury. Sara, although seething over the decision to serve such as "vulgar" treat to royalty, had little alternative but to acquiesce in her daughter-in-law's choice of food. All eyes were on the royal couple when Ostaghen brought the hot dogs round on a silver tray.

"How do I take it?" asked the King.

"Spear it," replied Ostaghen.[22]

The King did as he was told and then placed the hot dog in his left hand, covered it liberally with French mustard and placed it in his mouth. The Queen followed suit and then, to the delight of the other diners, they both asked for seconds. The King got further into the swing of things by washing his food down with two glasses of beer. After lunch, a man and woman in full Native American costume, complete with beads and feathers, staged an Indian programme. "Interesting," observed Suckley. "A little long perhaps."[23]

That afternoon, Roosevelt invited his guests to swim with him in the pool. The King accepted, but the Queen, much to Eleanor's regret, declined. "I had hoped the Queen would feel she could relax in the same way, but I discovered that if you were a queen you could not run the risk of looking dishevelled, so she and her lady-in-waiting sat by the side of the pool with me while the men were swimming," she recalled.[24]

Later, the President, who was sitting on the grass, wanted to move back into the shade, but no one was paying attention to him and so he started to propel himself backwards on his hands. "He was doing beautifully and gave himself a final big heave – right onto a tray of glasses & bottles," wrote Suckley.[25] The Queen told Eleanor Roosevelt that she hadn't the slightest idea that the President wasn't able to walk: they had just assumed he needed to use a cane.

There was also time during the day for more talks between the King and Roosevelt, though this time without Mackenzie

King. Again the subject was the impending war. As the King recorded in his notes of their conversation, there was some cause for optimism – even if it was soon to be proved tragically misplaced. "If London was bombed USA would come in," he said Roosevelt had told him, adding: "Offensive air warfare was better than defensive & he hoped we should do the same on Berlin." Roosevelt also suggested that the United States could help Britain in the event of war by carrying out sea and air patrols of the Atlantic from British bases in Trinidad, Bermuda and elsewhere in the Caribbean. There was talk, too, of Britain's massive outstanding debt from the previous war: "Debts. Better not reopen the question," the King wrote. "Congress wants repayment in full, which is impossible, & a small bit is of no use, as they will want more later."[26]

That evening they had dinner together again, but with the royal party due to leave at 10.40 p.m. in order to make their train, the mood was not as relaxed as it had been the previous evening. "There was that feeling one always gets of watching the clock and not becoming too involved in any conversation after dinner, for fear the hour of departure will arrive," Eleanor wrote in her column.

A procession of cars then drove from the house to the little Hyde Park station to see off the royal visitors. A crowd had gathered in the village and at the railway station, despite the heavy thunderstorm during dinner. The Queen remarked that after the ice and snow on their voyage and the heat of their stay, the downpour meant they had seen the complete cycle of weather. But the rain had stopped by the time they reached the station. The luggage and all the rest of the party were already on board, and the royal pair had said their goodbyes when the Queen abruptly turned back to Eleanor and asked to see the man who had been driving her husband during the trip. The man was produced, and she thanked him for the care with which he had driven.

The King and the Queen stood on the open rear platform of the train as it pulled out of the station, and the people who were gathered on the banks of the river slowly began to sing 'Auld Lang Syne'. "There was something incredibly moving about the scene – the river in the evening light, the voices of many people singing this old song, and the train slowly pulling out with the young couple waving goodbye," Eleanor recalled. "One thought of the clouds that hung over them and the worries they were going to face, and turned away and left the scene with a heavy heart."[27]

The Roosevelts were among those waving, but then Sara reminded them of an old superstition that said you should not watch people as they go out of sight. So, before the train had turned the bend, they got back into their cars and went home.

Although journalists were present at the station, they had been barred from the picnic, and forced to cover it from the pilot train in nearby Poughkeepsie, which formed a makeshift media centre. It was there they had been waiting during the afternoon for confirmation of the main news event of the day – perhaps even of the trip: whether the King had actually sampled the hot dog. To their dismay, they were initially told the weather had been so warm that hot dogs had not been served at all. Then came another briefing, at which it was announced that they had after all been on offer, but it was not known for sure whether or not the royal couple had partaken in the delicacy.

The situation was becoming serious. With deadlines looming, the journalists were getting desperate. There followed frantic calls to any official who might have the inside story on the goings-on at the picnic. It was only later in the evening that it was considered to have been definitively established that one dish of hot dogs had indeed been served.

The news was splashed over the front pages the next day, 12th June. "King Tries Hot Dog and Asks for More", proclaimed the *New York Times*. For the United Press news agency, whose reports were widely carried in the American papers, the real winner had been the hot dog itself. "The plebeian but succulent hot dog […] has enjoyed its greatest social triumph today," it declared. The King's performance also earned plaudits back home. "The King and Queen Eat Hot Dogs – and Ask for More", declared a headline in the *Daily Express*.

With obvious pride, the newspaper reported how the royal couple had resisted the temptation to reach for their knife and fork and "performed the ritual" of eating hot dogs just like Americans. "That simple little luncheon will enhance, if possible, the enormous popularity of the King and Queen already gained by their visit to Washington and their sensational welcome to New York yesterday," the *Express* declared. "If they can unbend sufficiently to eat a hot dog as an American would, that to an American is sure proof of their democratic qualities."

There was a curious postscript to the visit: overcoming her frugal nature, Sara had decided before the royal visit to buy from the local hardware shop a new lavatory seat for the bathroom that the Queen was going to use. After they had left, she had a change of heart and decided the old seat still had some life in it, after all. So she took the replacement back to the shop and demanded a credit be put on her account. The shopkeeper was just as tight-fisted as Sara, however, and initially refused before eventually backing down. He was determined not to be out of pocket, though, and displayed the item in his window with a "For Sale" sign and a mention of its royal connection. Word quickly got back to Sara, who had a change of mind and took back the seat.[28]

Chapter 14

Going Home

When the King and Queen woke the next morning, they found the *Royal Blue* train's tough-looking American police guards had been replaced by the familiar scarlet-coated Mounties. The temperature had also dropped sharply, thanks to an overnight storm that amounted to a minor cyclone. Their first stop back on Canadian soil was Sherbrooke, Quebec, known as the capital of the Eastern Townships, where one hundred thousand people turned out to meet them and proceeded to give them a welcome that would convince them they were once more back among their own. "The Americans are a fine lot of people and they gave Their Majesties a fine reception, but it's to us that the King and Queen belong," one patriotic Canadian told a reporter.[1]

A few more stops followed. After one in Rivière-du-Loup, the King invited Mackenzie King to his room; the latter found the monarch sitting on the sofa, reporter's notebook in hand. The King had written up in longhand an account of his conversations with Roosevelt and wanted to check with the Canadian that both had understood the President the same way.[2]

What did Mackenzie King think of Roosevelt's intentions? the King asked. Mackenzie replied that "it was clear to me that the President was anxious to do everything he possibly could to be of help, short of committing his country to a war".

The King concurred. "What a fine fellow he is," he said.

The King also noted how Roosevelt had made clear that he was "trying to educate the American people to appreciate what it would mean for them if Germany were to win a war, and the French and British forces to be wiped off the seas. They would then lose entirely their export market, and if they were given a chance to import into these countries, it would be wholly on the terms of the dictators themselves."

Reflecting on the American section of the trip, Mackenzie King assured the King it had surpassed all expectations. This had been apparent from the positive reaction of the crowds, which was "personal to himself and the Queen as well as expressive of sympathy with the British ideals of freedom and peace".

"This trip has made a great deal to me, and a great deal to the Queen," the King replied. He said it had been all about developing a "new idea of kingship" which was more in tune with the people and their interests – "no more the high-hat business, the kind of thing that my father and those of his day regarded as essential, as the correct attitude, that certain things could not be done, everything was to be just in such and such a way".

Mackenzie King thought the King should trust his own instinct in such matters. The trip, he said, "ought to give him an assurance with regard to freedom of action and [he should] not allow himself to be circumvented by Court restrictions".

Perhaps because of the informality of the setting, the King opened up on other matters, repeating his concerns about the possibility of Churchill eventually succeeding Chamberlain – a prospect he was not keen on himself and which he feared would not go down well with Roosevelt. He also described how uncomfortable he had been made to feel by Anthony Eden, who had resigned as Foreign Secretary the previous year, during audiences: whenever he asked him a question, the minister would reply by reading from a piece of paper rather than talking to him frankly man-to-man. Mackenzie King put it down to the superior manner Eden acquired at Oxford.

Most revealing, though, were the insights the King gave into his attitudes to the throne. "When my father was alive, he filled an important place, was much before the public," he told Mackenzie King. "My brother was equally prominent before the public. I was kept in the background. My father used to tell me I could never do anything because I could not speak." Indeed, before George V's death, when he could see the way things might go, he had gone to Sandringham with a view to telling his father he would not accept the throne – but never did so. That being said, he revealed that

George V had always been worried about how Edward would behave, especially after his performance during his two trips to America.

In the event, the future George VI had had no choice when his brother abdicated; but even then, more than two years into his reign, he clearly still felt insecure; he told Mackenzie King that "the press were continually saying that he knew very little about affairs; that he could not speak; was merely filling a place".

Mackenzie King, clearly touched, then mentioned the speech the King had made the previous evening and how it had gone so well he felt like standing up and cheering at the end. He told the King he should take advantage of chances that had presented themselves on the trip to speak whenever he wished. "If he did not feel like it, to say nothing, but if he did, to get up and say what he wished to say." The King smiled and said he "thought he could manage it".

The more they talked, the more it became clear how much of an impression the tour had made on the King – so much so that he revealed he was thinking of embarking on another, though this time to South America. His idea was that a ship similar to the *Empress of Australia* should be fitted out so he could use it whenever he wished to travel to any corner of the Empire, accompanied by appropriate officials able to brief him on the areas he visited. Mackenzie King was enthusiastic, though what the King's own government back in Britain would make of such a plan, with all its potential implications for royal interference in foreign policy, was not clear. In any case, events intruded and it never happened.

Later that day, as the *Royal Blue* train was running through the last of French Canada, the King sent Roosevelt a telegram thanking him for the welcome they had been given.

THE PRESIDENT.

The Queen and I are deeply grateful, Mr President, to Mrs Roosevelt and yourself for your hospitality during the past four days. The kindness shown to us personally by you both was endorsed by your fellow countrymen and countrywomen with a cordiality that has stirred our hearts. In Washington, in New York and indeed wherever we have been in the United States, we have been accorded a reception of which the friendliness was unmistakable. Though this was our first visit to your great country and though it was necessarily only a brief one, it has given us memories of kindly feeling and goodwill that we shall always treasure. To you, our host, and to the many thousands of American citizens who also showed us such true hospitality and such spontaneous courtesy, we send our heartfelt thanks and our best wishes.

GEORGE R.I.[3]

The next day was spent in New Brunswick, with stops at Newcastle, Fredericton, St John and Moncton. The following morning, 14th June, they crossed the nine-mile-wide Northumberland Strait to Prince Edward Island – to which the King had paid a three-day visit in 1913 when he was a naval cadet. The heat that had characterized the American leg of their journey was now a distant memory: the rain was so heavy that those attending a garden party at Government House in Charlottetown were obliged to don overcoats and mackintoshes. From there it was back across the strait to Pictou, a little harbour town whose population was almost entirely Scottish, and then a drive of a few miles to New Glasgow, where, just after eight o'clock, they boarded the *Royal Blue* for what was to be their last night.

Early the following morning, they made a brief stop in Truro, a settlement of eight thousand people. There they picked up Lord Tweedsmuir, who accompanied them for the final sixty-mile stretch of their journey to Halifax, where the *Empress of Britain* was waiting to carry them home. More than one hundred thousand people, crowded onto the dockside and along the streets of the city, broke into thunderous cheers as a twenty-one-gun salute crashed out from the fortress of Citadel Hill.

The time had come to leave the train. After a round of farewells to those who had served them during their journey backwards and forwards across Canada, the King and Queen set off by car on a one-mile drive through the brilliantly decorated streets of the city for a lunch at Province House. Then, speaking into three golden microphones hidden among the table decorations, the King made a farewell speech that was broadcast across the Empire. In it, he thanked the people of Canada – and of the country's "great and friendly neighbour to the south" – for the reception he and the Queen had received.

"You have given us a welcome of which the memory will always be dear to us," he said. "Our hearts and minds are full. We leave your shores after some of the most inspiring and illuminating weeks in our lives." The King also praised the Americas as "a large part of the earth where there is no possibility of war between neighbours, whose peoples are wholly dedicated to the pursuits of peace, a pattern to all men of how civilized nations should live together", adding, with a nod to the worsening situation in Europe: "By God's grace yours may yet be the example which all the world will follow."[4]

That evening, after another trip through the city and a private tea with the lieutenant governor, they drove down to the dockyard under a white archway emblazoned with the words "Goodbye to Nova Scotia" and boarded the ship. After the final farewells, the red-carpeted gangplank was removed, the hawsers were cast off and just after seven o'clock the ship began to move away. A cheer went up from the shore, and as the vessels in the harbour blew their sirens, the King and Queen went to the bridge to wave goodbye. And with that the great liner glided into the smooth waters of Halifax Harbour.

Waiting for them on the ship was a letter from Roosevelt:

I cannot allow you and the Queen to sail for home without expressing once more the extreme pleasure which your all too brief visit to the United States gave us.

The warmth of the welcome accorded you everywhere you visited in this country was the spontaneous outpouring of Americans who were deeply touched by the tact, the graciousness, and the understanding hearts of your guests.

I shall always like to think that you felt the sincerity of this manifestation of the friendship of the American people.

Mrs Roosevelt joins me in parting felicitations to Your Majesties and best wishes for a safe and pleasant voyage.

Franklin D. Roosevelt
(Initialled) FDR[5]

The crowds that greeted the King and Queen as they docked in Southampton on 22nd June and then travelled on to Waterloo were just as enthusiastic as they had been on the other side of the Atlantic, although a lot more deferential. The Britain to which they returned was one sliding inexorably towards war. Air-raid shelters were being dug and hundreds of barrage balloons had already been manufactured; preparations were well under way to evacuate children from London and other major cities.

That afternoon, Parliament met to pass an address of "loyal and affectionate welcome" to the King and Queen, prompted by Neville Chamberlain. The Prime Minister declared that the reception they had been given by the Canadians had shown how "loyalty to the Crown in the abstract has been translated into personal feeling of affection for Their Majesties". He was also keen to point to the warmth of their greeting by the Americans, which he claimed "both as a personal tribute to the King and Queen and as a striking proof of the sympathy and friendship which animate the feelings of the peoples of the United States and the United Kingdom".[6]

Arthur Greenwood, the deputy leader of the opposition Labour Party, went further: "If there be some who believed that this far-flung Empire with the King as its symbolic head is a myth, the visit of Their Majestics must have dispelled that view," he said. As for the welcome given the royal couple in America, "No words of mine are adequate to express what I believe to be the real significance of this visit. It may have more far-reaching results in maintaining peace and friendliness in the world than we know. For that we greet them back home amongst us".[7]

Both Houses then adjourned to allow members to hurry to the places that had been reserved for them in Parliament Square to watch the King and Queen make their way in an open landau the two miles from Waterloo to Buckingham Palace. Around a million people lined the route. According to one observer, the scenes "recalled those of the coronation, except that the people were much jollier, and the King and Queen seemed more happy and self-assured than ever before. The acclamation of the crowds, too, had a new depth of feeling, doubtless born of the tour's success and the adventures through which Their Majesties had passed."[8]

Back in Buckingham Palace, the King and Queen, along with their two daughters, came out onto the balcony and acknowledged the cheers from tens of thousands of people gathered outside. They stayed out five minutes before making a final wave and retiring inside. The crowd, just as had been the case in Canada and America, showed little sign of being ready to go home, however, and called for the King and Queen to come out again. Their patience was finally rewarded at 8.40 p.m., when they reappeared, the King in a double-breasted dinner jacket and the Queen in a blue evening gown.

The spectators stayed on for another three hours or more in the hope of catching a final glimpse of the royal couple. They were disappointed: instead, they saw Chamberlain arrive at half-past nine and stay for almost two hours to discuss the trip. By half-past eleven, the lights had gone out; after more than six weeks away, the King and Queen had finally gone to bed in their own home again.

The King needed his rest. The next day he was due to make a speech at a lunch at the Guildhall.[9] It was seen as a significant one, and its contents had been a major preoccupation for him during his tour. The King had cabled Logue from the ship the previous day to come to the Palace on the morning of the address. To Logue, he initially seemed nervous, but once he started to talk about the trip, he relaxed and broke into his characteristic grin. "He was most interested in Roosevelt – a most delightful man he called him," Logue wrote.

Some seven hundred of the great and the good were there to hear the King speak. They were treated to an eight-course lunch, washed down with two brands of 1928 champagne and vintage port. "It is a great pity that a colour film was not made of the scene," commented the *Daily Express*. "It would have preserved for posterity a close-up of the entire executive power of Britain, tightly packed on a few square yards of blue carpet."

Most of the speech was devoted to the Canadian chapter of the trip, with the King describing how the visit had underlined the strength of Britain's links with its Dominion. "In Canada, I saw everywhere not only the mere symbol of the British Crown; I saw also, flourishing strongly as they do here, the institutions which have developed, century after century, beneath the aegis of that Crown," he told his audience, who interrupted him several times with loud cheers. The great Commonwealth of Nations of which both countries were a part existed as "a potent force for promoting peace and goodwill among mankind", he noted.

Surprisingly perhaps, given its significance, the King made little mention of the American leg – an omission that Logue had pointed out during their run-through that morning, by which time it had been too late to change the text. Nor did he mention Roosevelt by name. He did, though, reflect on the warmth of the welcome he had received in America and noted the interest shown in the copy of the Magna Carta on display at the World's Fair in New York, which he said revealed "how closely interwoven are the threads of our own story with those of the development of that newer continent across the sea".

In the weeks that followed, the sense grew that a war was coming, especially after the signing on 23rd August of a non-aggression pact between Germany and the Soviet Union that was to give Hitler a free hand to invade Poland and then turn his forces to the west. Three days later, Britain signed a treaty with the government in Warsaw pledging to come to Poland's assistance if it were attacked. Chamberlain nevertheless continued to negotiate with Hitler, even though he turned down the King's offer to write a personal letter to the Nazi leader. For many people, though, the worst thing was the uncertainty.

So what had the royal trip actually achieved? The immediate reaction in the American media was overwhelmingly positive, thanks largely to the King and Queen's warmth and easygoing style. A summary of American press reports sent by Ronald Lindsay to the Foreign Secretary Lord Halifax on 20th June had noted with appreciation the sheer quantity of royal coverage and tracked how the wariness that had been expressed in some quarters ahead of the visit had given way to largely unbridled enthusiasm.[10]

The King and Queen had shown "how democratic and wholesome are the symbols of the constitutional monarchy that is Britain's", wrote Arthur Krock, the *New York Times*'s Pulitzer Prize-winning Washington-bureau chief as the royal couple arrived at Hyde Park. In another report summing up the visit, published as the royal couple left the United States two days later, the same paper described the warm welcome they had been given as "a genuine tribute [...] as much to the British people as to their sovereigns". It added: "We like the British because we understand them better than most foreigners. And, after all, why shouldn't we? They gave us our speech, our manners and our customs, and, after a little persuasion by the continental army, our country itself." The *Washington Post* was equally effusive in its praise: "To say that the King and Queen were received here with open arms would be an understatement," it said. "It was into the hearts of the population that they were taken, and taken without reservation." For the *Christian Science Monitor*, meanwhile, "the old bond between the democracies has taken on higher, warmer, yes, friendlier qualities than it ever had before."[11]

Other papers took a similar line, although there were some dissenting voices: Lindsay noted the attitude of the papers in the Midwest and on the Pacific coast had been "noticeably cooler" than in the East. Coolest of all was the *Chicago*

Tribune, which, out of hostility to Roosevelt, had from the start sought to pour cold water on the visit and "ridiculed those who attended the various ceremonies in Washington". The real aim of the visit, the newspaper claimed, had been to lure America out of its isolation into some form of alliance with Britain – a suggestion dismissed as ludicrous by most other papers. "Our isolationists can sleep just as soundly at night this week as they are accustomed to do when British heads are not in our midst spinning imaginary webs of entanglement," said the *Washington Star.* "The King and Queen are come to us purely and simply bearing the olive branch of a comradeship that has endured unbroken for nearly a century and a half."[12]

The *Chicago Tribune*'s carping apart, Ambassador Lindsay could therefore be pleased with what he read – and had witnessed. "The Royal visit which ended last night can only be characterized as a complete success," he wrote to Halifax. "There can be no doubt that the visit has made [*sic*] profound impression on the whole country and has deepened and fixed already existing feelings of friendliness. Coming at a crucial moment, it is of capital importance in the history of Anglo-American relations and its effects will not wear off."[13]

Sir Godfrey Haggard, the Consul General in New York, was also full of praise for what he called "the remarkable success of the royal visit". Thanks to their "natural friendly yet dignified bearing" the pair had revealed "British royalty in a guise which has surprised and delighted the man in the New York street", he wrote. "That there is a brain underneath Her Majesty's becoming hats, and genuine feeling behind His Majesty's handshake is a discovery that is going to promote a better understanding of Britain's system of government and Britain's problems, and help to consign to limbo legends current since the Abdication."[14]

There was also no doubting the positive effect that the enthusiastic response received by the royal couple had on the King's self-esteem. "The trip nowhere had more influence than on George VI himself," noted *Time* magazine in a report published several days after his return. "Two years ago he took on his job at a few hours' notice, having expected to play a quiet younger brother role to Brother Edward all his life. Pressmen who followed him around the long loop from Quebec to Halifax were struck by the added poise and self-confidence that George drew from the ordeal." Despite the difference in age and culture between the hosts and their guests, both couples had bonded. The Roosevelts, the magazine noted, had "developed a father-&-motherly feeling towards this nice young couple".[15]

Writing almost two decades later, the King's official biographer, John W. Wheeler-Bennett, agreed on the positive effect it had on him. The trip had "taken him out of himself, had opened up for him wider horizons and introduced him to new ideas", he noted. "It marked the end of his apprenticeship as a monarch, and gave him self-confidence and assurance. No longer was he overawed by the magnitude of his responsibility, the greatness of his office and the burden of its traditions. Now at last, he felt, he could stand on his own feet and trust his own judgement."[16]

It was one thing for the American press – and officialdom from the President downwards – to warm to their royal visitors. Persuading Congress, and Americans as a whole, to give up isolationism in favour of a potential alliance with Britain in the forthcoming conflict was a completely different matter, as Lindsay and others involved on the British side readily acknowledged. Despite the warmth of the reception given to the royal couple, the "results in the immediate future specifically as regards legislation on neutrality are more doubtful", Lindsay admitted, noting that a hard core of isolationists in the Senate would remain determined to resist attempts by the administration to pass amendments to the Neutrality Act. "But it is quite certain that the royal visit will have greatly increased the pressure in the opposite direction [...] In other words, while we cannot at present feel certain of receiving an immediate dividend we can be assured that our hidden reserves have been immensely strengthened."

Chapter 15

War

On Sunday 3rd September 1939, the inevitable finally happened: Sir Nevile Henderson, the British ambassador to Berlin, delivered a final note to the German government. In it he stated that unless Hitler withdrew the troops he had sent into Poland two days earlier by 11 a.m. that day, Britain would declare war. No such undertaking was given. At 11.15 a.m. Chamberlain announced in sorrowful and heartfelt tones that Britain was now at war with Germany. France followed a few hours later.

Canada did not immediately join them. In 1914, as a quasi-independent Dominion, it had automatically gone to war along with the mother country, and some commentators insisted that the same should happen this time, since the declaration of war had been made by their monarch. Mackenzie King thought otherwise. The 1931 Statute of Westminster had turned Canada into a fully sovereign state and, as he repeatedly declared: "Parliament will decide." And so the Canadian House of Commons was called in special session.

The resolution to declare war was put forward by Ernest Lapointe, the francophone minister of justice, who drew on the royal visit. As the royal couple had left, the Queen had said farewell with a blessing: "*Que Dieu bénisse le Canada*" ("God bless Canada"). Lapointe closed his speech with her words. It had the desired effect: although a small group of parliamentarians from Quebec tried to amend the bill, it passed by acclamation on 9th September. The Senate approved it the same day. That night the Cabinet drafted a declaration of war, which Lord Tweedsmuir signed on 10th September. Earlier hopes of a "limited" involvement were to prove an illusion. Between 1939 and 1945 almost 1.1 million Canadians – more than forty per cent of the male population between the ages of eighteen and forty-five – enlisted; virtually all of them were volunteers. More than forty-five thousand were killed.

The United States necessarily found itself in a different position. Two days before Britain declared war on Germany, as Nazi forces were advancing into Poland, Roosevelt had met a group of journalists in the Oval Office.

"Can we stay out of this?" one of them demanded.

"I not only sincerely hope so, but I believe we can and every effort will be made by this administration so to do," Roosevelt replied. He reiterated that point on the evening of 3rd September in his fireside chat. "This nation will remain a neutral nation, but I cannot ask that every American remain neutral in thought as well," he told the nation. "Even a neutral has a right to take account of facts. Even a neutral cannot be asked to close his mind or his conscience."[1]

However warm the relationship that had developed between King and President, there could be no question of America joining the fighting on the British side – for the time being, at least. Although polls showed at least seventy-five per cent of Americans favoured the Allied cause that September, at least ninety-five per cent were equally fervently opposed to America's becoming "involved in Europe's wars". Nor did that change soon – on the contrary. The period of inactivity during the first few months of the so-called "Phoney War" led some in the US government to question the seriousness of the British and French resolve in fighting the Nazis. Then the Allied disasters of April, May and June 1940, when the Germans swept through Western Europe, convinced many that Hitler's forces were indeed invincible – further strengthening the feeling that America should steer well clear. One of the most notorious proponents of such a view was Ambassador Joseph Kennedy, whose position became increasingly isolationist, to the anger of his British hosts and the embarrassment of Roosevelt. He was eventually forced to resign from his post in November 1940 after an interview with the *Boston Sunday Globe* in which he declared: "Democracy is finished in England. It may be here."

Armed intervention by the United States may have been out of the question, but a movement to aid Britain "by all means short of war" grew as Americans came to realize the danger that the Nazis might also ultimately pose to their continent.

Admiration grew, too, for the determination with which the British, despised by many for their appeasement of Hitler in the run-up to the outbreak of war, were prepared to fight on, if necessary alone. The courage of the King and Queen – and their willingness to remain in London as German bombs rained down on the city – added to the feelings of sympathy.

So what of the friendship that had developed between the King and Roosevelt during their short time together? For George VI's official biographer, there is little doubt that their meeting, however brief, helped encourage the Anglo-American alliance that was to be forged between the President and Winston Churchill after the latter became prime minister in May 1940 following the resignation of Chamberlain. The King and Queen, Wheeler-Bennett wrote, had, "in the course of their visit to the United States in the summer of 1939, disclosed to the American public the essential fact that 'royalty' are 'people', and in three days did more to demolish anti-British feeling in America than could have been achieved in a quarter of a century of diplomatic manoeuvring. Theirs was the foundation upon which others builded [sic]; theirs the spark which others tended into flame."[2]

The warmth of this relationship was reflected in the letters Roosevelt and the King began to exchange in the spring of 1940. In one, dated 1st May, the President looked back to their time together at his country house. "Last June seems years distant," he wrote to the King. "You will remember that the Saturday night at Hyde Park when I kept you up, after a strenuous day, I may have seemed pessimistic in my belief in the probability of war. More than a month after that I found the Congress assured that there would be no war, and for a few weeks I had to accept the charge of being a 'calamity-howler'."

"I certainly do not rejoice in my prophecies," he continued, "but at least it has given me opportunity to bring home the seriousness of the world situation to the type of American who has hitherto believed, in much too large numbers, that no matter what happens there will be little effect on this country." Roosevelt then added a personal note showing his genuine affection for the royal couple: "Always I want you and your family to know that you have very warm friends in my wife and myself over here, and you must not hesitate to call on me for any possible thing if I can help or lighten your load."[3]

At this stage, though, what the King – and his country – really needed was not sympathy but arms: on 1st June 1940, Roosevelt had heeded a request from Churchill and authorized the sale of munitions worth $37 million to replace those lost during the evacuation of Dunkirk. Churchill followed this up by asking him to provide Britain with destroyers too: the Royal Navy was down to its last sixty-eight vessels, which it needed not just to defend its trade routes against German U-boat attacks but also to guard against the danger of invasion. Only America could help.

The King weighed in with a personal letter to the President in which he reminisced about "the delightful days" they had spent the previous June. After talking of the magnificent spirit, resolution and confidence shown by his fellow Britons in the face of the Nazi assault, the King got to the point: "As you know, we are in urgent need of some of your older destroyers to tide us over the next few months," he wrote. "I well understand your difficulties and I am certain that you will do your best to procure them for us before it is too late. Now that we have been deprived of the assistance of the French Fleet – to put the least unfavourable interpretation on the present position – the need is becoming greater every day if we are to carry on our solitary fight for freedom to a successful conclusion."[4]

The request put Roosevelt in an awkward position: it was difficult to reconcile the transfer of fifty destroyers to Britain with American neutrality; there was even the danger Hitler might consider it a *casus belli*. There was also the problem of how Congress would react: it had recently ruled that no military property could be transferred to a foreign country unless it had been previously certified as surplus to the needs of the service involved. Despite this, Roosevelt was prepared to accede to the request, but he also wanted something in return: namely to link provision of the ships with the plan that he and the King had discussed at Hyde Park to allow the Americans to use British bases in the Caribbean and the north Atlantic. Churchill was reluctant to make such a link, but Roosevelt insisted this was the only way he could sell the deal to Congress. Churchill finally accepted and an agreement was reached on 2nd September: Britain acquired fifty reconditioned destroyers, and the Americans were granted ninety-nine-year leases that would allow them to establish air and sea bases in Newfoundland, Bermuda, the Bahamas, Jamaica, Antigua, St Lucia, Trinidad and British Guiana.

The King hailed the deal in a letter he sent to Roosevelt three days later: "The friendly action of the United States in making these all-important ships available for us has evoked a warm feeling of gratitude throughout this country, and we hope that our offer of facilities in the western Atlantic for the defence of North America will give equal satisfaction to your people," he wrote. "I remember so well the talk we had on this particular subject at Hyde Park – but how far off all that seems now!"[5]

Yet, however warm the relationship between King and President – and, indeed, between their respective countries – there was still no chance of America actually entering the war. A few days after the agreement was signed, the Germans began an eight-month bombing campaign against British cities that became known as the Blitz, but Roosevelt showed no sign of making good on his promise at Hyde Park that if London were bombed, the United States would come in. Nor did the President's re-election for a third term in November 1940 immediately change the situation: the mandate he had received from voters was for "all aid short of war"; however liberally he interpreted this, he knew that he had the support of neither Congress nor the American people to fight side by side with Britain against the Nazis.

On the positive side, though, the following month, after a special message from Roosevelt, the House of Representatives passed a bill to amend the Neutrality Act to allow US merchantmen to sail to war zones. The American Atlantic patrols that the King and the President discussed at Hyde Park were finally getting under way.

In the months that followed, there was more good news from Washington: the "Lend-Lease" legislation passed by Congress in March 1941 allowed Britain, which was rapidly running out of dollar assets, to continue to obtain much-needed arms from America, which had hitherto been available only on a "cash-and-carry basis". Although the move was controversial, it showed quite how far relations between the two countries had moved since the start of the war. Then, in May, Roosevelt proclaimed an "unlimited state of national emergency" that authorized US warships escorting supply vessels bound for Britain to defend themselves against enemy attack – raising the prospect of America becoming embroiled in a shooting war.

In a letter that June, the King made yet another reference to their conversation at Hyde Park. "After so many years of anxiety, when what we wanted to happen seemed so far from realization, it is wonderful to feel that at last our two great countries are getting together for the future betterment of the world," he wrote.[6]

Ultimately, though, the final impetus that drove America into the war came not from Europe but from Asia. On the morning of 7th December 1941, US time, the Japanese attacked Pearl Harbor: after just two hours of bombing, more than 2,400 Americans were dead, twenty-one ships had either been sunk or damaged and 188 US aircraft destroyed. The next day Roosevelt gave an address to Congress in which he declared the day of the attack was "a date that will live in infamy". At the end of the speech, he asked Congress to approve a declaration of war on Japan. The Senate and House of Representatives did so almost unanimously – with only one vote against, by Jeannette Rankin, a pacifist congresswoman. When Germany and Italy responded three days later by declaring war on America under the terms of their alliance with Japan, Congress declared war on them too.

The catastrophe at Pearl Harbor coincided with more bad news for the British: attacks on Hong Kong and Malaya and the sinking of the great battleship *Prince of Wales* and the battlecruiser *Repulse*. Yet it meant Britain was no longer fighting alone. The King was quick to write to Roosevelt. "My thoughts and prayers go out to you and to the great people of the United States at this solemn moment in your history when you have been treacherously attacked by Japan," he wrote. "We are proud indeed to be fighting at your side against the common enemy. We share your inflexible determination, your confidence that with God's help the power of darkness will be overcome and the four freedoms established throughout a world purged of tyranny."[7] But it would take almost four more years of fighting, in which both countries – and Canada, too – suffered appalling losses, before that common enemy was defeated.

When the King and Queen left Hyde Park, they had urged the President and his wife to pay a return visit to Britain. Although the outbreak of war necessarily meant a postponement, it was a message that was repeated by Churchill during the several meetings he had with Roosevelt after he became prime minister. Such a meeting, however, would have to wait for victory – which was still a long way off.

In the meantime, it was decided that Eleanor, who had remained in contact with the Queen, could travel to Britain on her own; the declared purpose was for her to be able to see at first hand the part women were playing in the war effort and to visit American troops stationed in Britain. It would also be rich in symbolism, serving as a sign of the strength of relations between the two countries. "I wish much that I could accompany her, for there are a thousand things I want to tell you and talk with you about," the President wrote to the King.[8]

Eleanor's visit, which took place in October 1942, was an undoubted success – and one that brought home to the First Lady the extent to which the King and Queen were sharing the privations of the British people. The contrast with their time at Hyde Park could not have been greater: the vast rooms of Buckingham Palace were cold and damp, some of the windows were boarded up as a result of bombing, while the food on offer, at a time of rationing, was appropriately modest – even though it was served somewhat incongruously on gold and silver plates. The King and Queen personally took Eleanor on a tour of London to see the devastating aftermath of the Blitz. Their first stop was St Paul's Cathedral; they then went on to the East End.

After Eleanor had left, the King wrote to Roosevelt to say what a pleasure it had been to receive his wife. "That she should have made the long journey in these dangerous war days has touched and delighted our people and they are very glad to welcome her here," he said. He also expressed the wish that he and the President would be able to talk things over again in person, adding: "Let us hope this will be possible sooner than we think."[9] Eleanor herself wrote later of how her experiences in Britain had reinforced the respect she felt for the King and Queen. "The feeling I had had about them during their visit to the United States, that they were simply a young and charming couple, who would have to undergo some very difficult experiences, began to come back to me, intensified by the realization that they now had been through these experiences and were anxious to tell me about them," she recorded in her autobiography.[10]

The King continued to hope that Roosevelt himself could come to Britain – a hope that seemed to have a good chance of becoming reality as the tide of the war gradually turned in the Allies' favour. At the Yalta Conference in February 1945, which brought Roosevelt together with Churchill and Stalin, the idea was mooted that the President travel that April to San Francisco to attend the opening session of the United Nations and then on some time in late May or early June to Europe, visiting Britain and then France, the Netherlands and the Front. By that time, the President confidently predicted, the war would be over. The high point would be a stay at Buckingham Palace.

Roosevelt, Churchill declared, would "get from the British people the greatest reception ever accorded to any human being since Lord Nelson made his triumphant return to London". The King, for his part, was delighted at the prospect of welcoming as his guest a man who, by now, he had come to consider an old friend. "We shall do our best to make you comfortable here and it would be a real pleasure to the Queen and myself to have you with us and to continue that friendship which started so happily in Washington & at Hyde Park in 1939," he wrote to the President. "So much has happened to us all since those days."[11]

It was not to be, however. Although Roosevelt was aged just sixty-three and full of plans for the future, his health was deteriorating badly. During a long weekend at Hyde Park that March, Eleanor noted sadly that her husband no longer wanted to drive around the grounds in his Ford, letting her take the wheel instead – something he had never done before. He even allowed her to mix the cocktails, which would have been inconceivable just a few months earlier. On 29th March, looking drawn and grey, he returned from Hyde Park to Washington only to set off later that day to Warm Springs, Georgia, for a two-week rest, accompanied by Daisy Suckley and another cousin, Laura Delano. Also to be present at the house was Lucy Rutherfurd. Eleanor, however, did not go with him.

On the afternoon of 12th April 1945, while sitting for a portrait by Elizabeth Shoumatoff, Roosevelt became confused and raised his left hand shakily to his forehead. His head slumped forward. "I have a terrific pain in the back of my head," he told Suckley. He then fell unconscious and was carried to his bedroom. Dr Howard Bruenn, his attending cardiologist, diagnosed a large cerebral haemorrhage. At 3.35 p.m. he died.

Roosevelt had still so much more he planned to do once his fourth term ended in 1948, both on the world stage and in his personal life. Eleanor was the key to both. The previous Christmas, while driving with his son Elliott around Hyde Park, the President spoke of his desire to become reacquainted with his wife. "Father spoke to me about Mother in terms I had never heard him use before," Elliott recalled. "'You know,' he said, 'I think that Mother and I might be able to get together now and do things together, take some trips maybe, learn to know each other again.'"[12]

Mourners lined the railway tracks as Roosevelt's coffin was carried the eight hundred miles north from Warm Springs to Washington DC. After a funeral service in the East Wing of the White House, he was laid to rest in the rose garden of his beloved Springwood. In Britain, a week of mourning was ordered at court and the King cabled Eleanor to express his condolences. "The Queen and I are deeply grieved and shocked by the news of President Roosevelt's death," the King wrote. "In him humanity has lost a great figure and we have lost a true and honoured friend."[13]

The King, although just forty-nine when the war ended, was not well: the stress of the conflict, coupled with a lifetime of heavy smoking, had taken its toll. This did not prevent him from setting off in February 1947 on another royal tour: a gruelling ten-week visit to South Africa. In the years that followed, his health deteriorated further. An arterial blockage in 1948 prompted fears he might have to have his right leg amputated in order to avoid gangrene; instead, he had an operation to free the flow of blood to the limb. Then, in September 1951, he had a malignant tumour removed from his lung. He appeared to recover and went on, as usual, to spend that Christmas and New Year at Sandringham; during his time there he was even well enough to go out shooting. On the morning of 6th February 1952 he was found by a servant dead in his bed. The cause of death was not his cancer but rather a coronary thrombosis – a blood clot to the heart – that he had suffered soon after falling asleep.

George VI was the first reigning monarch to visit the United States, but he would not be the last: since succeeding her father in 1952, the present Queen has crossed the Atlantic three times: in 1957, 1976 and 1991. The trips have reflected the different spirits of the respective ages in which they have taken place.

The first visit, which followed the debacle of Suez, was timed to mark the 350th anniversary of the founding of the State of Virginia. It was also a clear attempt to revive the Anglophile sentiments seen during the King's time at Hyde Park: in her speeches during the ten-day visit, which followed a brief stop in Canada, the Queen repeatedly stressed – and hailed – the deep ties between Britain and America. In Washington, a million people braved the rain to watch her and Prince Philip drive from the airport to the White House. Harold Macmillan, the Prime Minister, spoke approvingly of the "the warmth and gaiety of the welcome given to the Queen by her subjects and our allies across the sea".[14]

Anglo-American relations were back on a much firmer footing when the Queen returned almost two decades later to mark the bicentenary of the War of American Independence. In a carefully worded speech in Philadelphia, she won plaudits from her hosts by praising the Founding Fathers for "having taught Britain a very valuable lesson": namely, knowing when it was time to bow to the desire of subjects to govern themselves. "Without that great act in the cause of liberty, performed in Independence Hall two hundred years ago, we could never have transformed an empire into a commonwealth," the Queen declared.[15]

If anything, the Queen received an even more enthusiastic welcome on her third visit which, taking place just three months after the victory of the US-led forces in the first Gulf War, underlined the continued strength of the special relationship between the two countries. She travelled widely, visiting Texas and Miami, as well as making the obligatory trip to Mount Vernon. She also notched up a number of firsts – among them holding the first royal receiving line at a baseball match and addressing a joint meeting of the United States Congress, a privilege that her father had been offered, but declined.

Where the Queen led, other members of the royal family have followed, notably Prince Charles, who visited in 1970 with Princess Anne and in 1985 with Diana, when *Time* hailed them as "the world's most glamorous and relentlessly observed twosome", while the *New York Times* reported simply: "The British have landed and Washington is taken."[16] The trip confirmed Diana's trajectory on the path towards international celebrity status, but the jubilant welcome she and Charles received was tempered by rumours that their marriage was in trouble. When Diana crossed the Atlantic again in 1989, it was on her own.

Such trips – coupled with state visits to Britain by President John F. Kennedy in 1961 and Ronald Reagan in 1982 – have added glitter to Anglo-American relations, helping them remain solid throughout the intervening decades. Yet no visit in either direction has quite recaptured the intimacy of that weekend in June 1939, when the Roosevelts welcomed the Queen's mother and father to their family home. All of which makes the friendship between King and President forged one hot summer afternoon over hot dogs and cocktails unique.

List of Abbreviations

AER   Eleanor Roosevelt, *The Autobiography of Eleanor Roosevelt* (New York, NY: Harper & Brothers, 1961).

AKS   The Duke of Windsor, *A King's Story* (London: Cassell, 1951).

CC   Geoffrey C. Ward, ed., *Closest Companion. The Unknown Story of the Intimate Friendship between Franklin Roosevelt and Margaret Suckley* (Boston, MA: Houghton Mifflin, 1995).

COB   William Shawcross, *Counting One's Blessings: The Selected Letters of Queen Elizabeth the Queen Mother* (London: Macmillan, 2012).

DMK   *The Diaries of William Lyon Mackenzie King* [www.collectionscanada.gc.ca/databases/king/].

EAC   Frank Prochaska, *The Eagle and the Crown: Americans and the British Monarchy* (New Haven, CT: Yale University Press, 2008).

FAL   Joseph E. Persico, *Franklin and Lucy: President Roosevelt, Mrs Rutherfurd, and the Other Remarkable Women in His Life* (New York, NY: Random House, 2008).

FDR:CF   Conrad Black, *Franklin Delano Roosevelt, Champion of Freedom* (New York, NY: Public Affairs, 2003).

GVI:HLR   John W. Wheeler-Bennett, *King George VI: His Life and Reign* (London: Macmillan, 1958).

KS   Mark Logue and Peter Conradi, *The King's Speech: How One Man Saved the British Monarchy* (London: Quercus, 2010).

NAS   Keith V. Gordon, *North America Sees Our King and Queen* (London: Hutchinson & Co., 1939).

PRO FO   Foreign Office files in Public Record Office, London.

RR   Will Swift, *The Roosevelts and the Royals* (Hoboken, NJ: John Wiley & Sons, 2004).

RWD   Elliott Roosevelt and James Brough, *A Rendezvous with Destiny: The Roosevelts of the White House* (New York, NY: Putnam, 1975).

TIR   Eleanor Roosevelt, *This I Remember* (New York, NY: Praeger, 1975).

VOS   G. Gordon Young, *Voyage of State* (London: Hodder & Stoughton, 1939).

Notes

CHAPTER 1

1 *New York Times*, 9th June 1939.
2 Ibid.
3 *RWD*, p. 148.
4 *RR*, p. 36.

CHAPTER 2

1 Sarah Bradford, *The Reluctant King: The Life and Reign of King George VI 1895–1952* (London: St Martin's Press, 1990), p. 18.
2 Quoted ibid., p. 22.
3 John Pudney, *His Majesty King George VI: A Study* (London: Hutchinson, 1952), p. 23.
4 *AKS*, p. 49.
5 Quoted in *KS*, p. 55.
6 Quoted ibid., p. 56.
7 Quoted in Robert Rhodes James, *A Spirit Undaunted: The Political Role of George VI* (London: Little Brown, 1998), p. 92.

8   *COB*, p. 88.

9   Quoted in *GVI:HLR*, p. 207.

10 Quoted ibid., p. 208.

11 Taylor Darbyshire, *The Duke of York* (London: Hutchinson & Co., 1929), p. 90.

12 Quoted in *KS*, p. 67.

13 Quoted in *GVI:HLR*, p. 230.

14 Quoted in *KS*, p. 131.

CHAPTER 3

1   *TIR*, p. 184.

2   *FDR:CF*, p. 522.

3   Quoted in *RR*, p. 71.

4   'Vade Mecum 1939' (*PRO FO* A3880/27/45).

5   Quoted in Janet Adam Smith, *John Buchan: A Biography* (London: Rupert Hart-Davis, 1965), p. 451.

6   Quoted in Martyn Cornick, 'War, Culture and the British Royal Visit to Paris, July 1938', *Synergies Royaume-Uni et Irlande*, No. 4 (2011), p. 152.

7   The *Daily Express* editorial was quoted in, among others, the *Pittsburgh Press*, 9th February 1938.

8   *New York Times*, 24th July 1938.

9   President Roosevelt to King George VI, 17th September 1938, President Franklin D. Roosevelt Presidential Library and Museum [docs.fdrlibrary.marist.edu/INVITAT. HTML].

10 Quoted in *GVI:HLR*, p. 373.

11 Ronald Lindsay to Alexander Hardinge, 25th October 1938 (*PRO FO* A8061).

12 Lady Reading to Lord Halifax, 16th February 1939 (*PRO FO* A1406/27/45).

13 Quoted in the *Canberra Times*, 24th October 1938.

14 *PRO FO* 371/22799/174.

15 *Milwaukee Journal*, 4th November 1938.

16 Associated Press in *Lewiston Morning Tribune*, 26th February 1939.

17 Associated Press in *News and Courier*, 11th December 1938.

18 'Selling George VI to the US', *Scribner's Magazine* (February 1939), p. 16.

19 *PRO FO* 371/22799/213.

20 Sir Eric Mieville to Charles Peake, 1st February 1939 (*PRO FO* A1665/27/45).

21 *Milwaukee Journal*, 18th February 1939.

22 President Roosevelt to King George VI, 18th January 1939 (*PRO FO* 371/22799/223).

23 Helen Woods to Lady Reading, 6th February 1939 (*PRO FO* 371/22799/233).

24 Frederick Hoyer Millar to J. Balfour, 17th February 1939 (*PRO FO* 371/22799/243).

25 A. Beckett to J. Balfour, 6th January 1939 (*PRO FO* 371/22799/152).

26 *GVI:HLR*, p. 375.

27 Ibid.

28 James Roosevelt, *My Parents: A Different View* (Chicago, IL: Playboy Press, 1976), p. 209.

29 Quoted in Peter Collier and David Horowitz, *The Kennedys, An American Dream* (New York, NY: Summit Books, 1984), p. 80.

30 *FDR:CF*, p. 439.

31 Quoted in Michael Beschloss, *Kennedy and Roosevelt: The Uneasy Alliance* (New York, NY: Norton, 1980), p. 187.

CHAPTER 4

1 *RR*, p 11.

2 *FDR:CF*, p. 145.

3 Quoted in Joseph Alsop, *FDR: A Centenary Remembrance* (New York, NY: Random House, 1985), p. 41.

4 *FAL*, p. 22.

5 Quoted in Joseph P. Lash, *Love, Eleanor: Eleanor Roosevelt and Her Friends* (New York, NY: McGraw-Hill, 1985), p. 26.

6 *FAL*, p. 55.

7 Quoted in *FAL*, p. 71.

8 *FAL*, p. 11.

9 Quoted in Joseph P. Lash, *Love, Eleanor: Eleanor Roosevelt and Her Friends* (New York, NY: McGraw-Hill, 1985), p. 72.

10 *FAL*, p. 129.

11 Ralph G. Martin, *Cissy: The Extraordinary Life of Eleanor Medill Patterson* (New York, NY: Simon & Schuster, 1979), p. 360.

12 Rodger Streitmatter, ed., *Empty without You: The Intimate Letters of Eleanor Roosevelt and Lorena Hickok* (New York, NY: Simon & Schuster, 1998), p. xix.

13 *FAL*, p. 205.

14 Arthur Schlesinger Jr and Franklin D. Roosevelt Jr were quoted in *People*, 12th November 1979.

CHAPTER 5

1   *CC*, p. xi.

2   Ibid., p. xiii.

3   Ibid., p. xvii.

4   The quotations from Daisy Suckley's diary in this and the following paragraph are found in *CC*, pp. 4–5.

5   Ibid., p. 34.

6   Ibid., p. 35.

7   Ibid., p. 61.

8   Ibid., p. 65.

9   Ibid., p. 67.

10 Ibid., p. 99.

11 Ibid., p. 101.

12 John Lloyd Wright and the Middletown architect were quoted in the *New York Times*, 14th June 2001.

13 Ibid.

14 Ibid.

15 *FAL*, p. 252.

16 Ibid., p. 145.

17 *RWD*, p. 45.

18 Quoted in *FAL*, p. 240.

19 Quoted in the *New York Times*, 27th May 1976.

20 Quoted ibid., 31st August 1989.

21 *FAL*, p. 215.

CHAPTER 6

1   *NAS*, p. 4.

2   The quotations from Lionel Logue in this and the following paragraph are found in *KS*, pp. 151–52.

3   *COB*, p. 263.

4   Ibid.

5   Ibid., p. 161.

6   *VOS*, p. 41.

7   Quoted ibid., p. 54.

8   *COB*, p. 264.

9   *VOS*, p. 55.

10 Quoted in *GVI:HLR*, p. 378.

11 Quoted in the *Pittsburgh Post-Gazette*, 9th May 1939 (and many other papers).

12 Quoted in Philip Ziegler, *King Edward VIII* (London: Collins, 1990), p. 399.

CHAPTER 7

1   *NAS*, p. 30.
2   Ibid., p. 47.
3   'America and the King', *The Spectator*, 19th May 1939.
4   J.V. Perowne, 19th May 1939 (*PRO FO* A3670/27/45).
5   *COB*, p. 269.
6   Quoted in *NAS*, p. 68.
7   *COB*, p. 268.
8   Quoted in *Maclean's*, 26th January 2011.
9   Quoted in the *Ottawa Citizen*, 25th May 1939 (and many other papers).
10 Quoted in *Maclean's*, 26th January 2011.
11 Quoted in *KS*, p. 153.
12 *NAS*, p. 89.
13 Ibid., p. 92.

CHAPTER 8

1   *DMK*, p. 633.
2   Ibid.
3   *VOS*, p. 202.
4   *DMK*, p. 642.
5   *NAS*, p. 131.
6   *VOS*, p. 211.
7   *DMK*, p. 643.

8 *VOS*, p. 214.

9 Ibid., p. 216.

10 Ibid.

11 *DMK*, p. 656.

12 *New York Times*, 8th June 1939.

13 *The Northern Miner*, 8th June 1939

CHAPTER 9

1 *EAC*, p. 4.

2 Ibid., p. 45.

3 Christopher Hibbert, *Edward VII: A Portrait* (New York, NY: Palgrave Macmillan, 2007), p. 31.

4 Quoted in Jane Ridley, *Bertie: A Life of Edward VII* (London: Chatto & Windus, 2012), p. 49.

5 Quoted ibid., p. 48.

6 *Harper's Weekly*, 18th August 1860.

7 *Los Angeles Times*, 24th January 1901.

8 *New York Times*, 19th July 1914.

9 *EAC*, p. 129.

10 Quoted ibid., p. 131.

11 *AKS*, p. 187.

12 Quoted in Philip Ziegler, *King Edward VIII* (London: Collins, 1990), p. 150.

13 *AKS*, p. 188.

14 *Morning Leader*, 13th October 1924.

15 *AKS*, p. 190.

16 *Washington Post*, 13th December 1936.

17 *Meriden Daily Journal*, 12th December 1936.

18 *San Jose News*, 18th May 1939.

CHAPTER 10

1   Quoted in *VOS*, p. 220.

2   Ibid., p. 222.

3   *AER*, p. 200.

4   Ibid., p. 199.

5   *TIR*, p. 183.

6   *AER*, p. 200.

7   *RWD*, p. 231.

8   Ibid., p. 232.

9   Ibid., pp. 149, 232.

10 All of the quotations from Eleanor Roosevelt in this and the following paragraphs are from *AER*, pp. 200–201.

11 All of Eleanor Roosevelt's 'My Day' columns can be read on the website of the George Washington University's Eleanor Roosevelt Papers Project [www.gwu.edu/~erpapers/myday/].

12 Quoted in Joseph P. Lash, *Eleanor and Franklin: The Story of Their Relationship, Based on Eleanor Roosevelt's Private Papers* (New York, NY: W. W. Norton & Company, 1971), p. 753.

13 Quoted in William Turner Levy and Cynthia Eagle Russett, *The Extraordinary Mrs R: A Friend Remembers*

Eleanor Roosevelt (New York, NY: John Wiley & Sons, 1999), p. 168.

CHAPTER 11

1 *Independent St Petersburg*, 31st May 1939.
2 *DMK*, p. 665.
3 Grace Tully, *FDR: My Boss* (New York, NY: Scribner, 1949), p. 317.
4 *TIR*, p. 188.
5 The quotations in this and the following two paragraphs are ibid., pp. 190–91.
6 *VOS*, p. 227.
7 *RWD*, p. 235.
8 Ibid., p. 235.
9 Quoted in the *New York Times*, 9th June 1939 (and many other papers).
10 Ronald Lindsay to Scott, 9th May 1939 (*PRO FO* A3524).
11 *DMK*, p. 667.
12 *RR*, p. 119.
13 Quoted in *VOS*, p. 233.
14 *New York Times*, 9th June 1939.
15 Quoted in *VOS*, p. 235.
16 Quoted ibid.
17 *NAS*, p. 197.
18 *VOS*, p. 234.
19 Quoted in *NAS*, pp. 197–98.

CHAPTER 12

1   The various newspapers were quoted in *Sydney Morning Herald*, 10th June 1939.

2   *NAS*, p. 202.

3   Ibid., p. 208.

4   *NAS*, p. 211.

5   Ibid., p. 211.

6   Quoted in *VOS*, p. 247.

7   Much of the information in this section is found in David J. Hope, 'King George and Queen Elizabeth's Visit to the Fair' [www.1939nyworldsfair.com/worlds_fair/wf_tour/zone-1/King_Queen.htm].

8   *New York Times*, 11th June 1939.

CHAPTER 13

1   *GVI:HLR*, p. 386.

2   *AER*, p. 206.

3   *CC*, p. 131.

4   *DMK*, p. 677.

5   *CC*, p. 131.

6   *AER*, p. 206.

7   *CC*, p. 132.

8   'Vade Mecum 1939' (*PRO FO* A3880/27/45).

9   *DMK*, p. 678.

10   'Transcript of King George VI's Handwritten Notes for a Memorandum on His Conversations with President

Roosevelt on June 10 and 11, 1939', President Franklin D. Roosevelt Presidential Library and Museum (docs. fdrlibrary.marist.edu/memorand.html).

11 *DMK*, p. 679.

12 Ibid.

13 *AER*, p. 207.

14 Quoted in *RWD*, p. 235.

15 *DMK*, p. 680.

16 All of the quotations from Daisy Suckley in this and the following paragraphs are from *CC*, p. 130.

17 *VOS*, p. 255.

18 *COB*, p. 271.

19 *DMK*, p. 681.

20 Quoted in *FDR:CF*, p. 524.

21 *COB*, p. 271.

22 *Daily Express*, 12th June 1939.

23 *CC*, p. 131.

24 *AER*, p. 207.

25 *CC*, p. 132.

26 'Transcript of King George VI's Handwritten Notes for a Memorandum on His Conversations with President Roosevelt on June 10 and 11, 1939', President Franklin D. Roosevelt Presidential Library and Museum (docs. fdrlibrary.marist.edu/memorand.html).

27 *AER*, p. 207.

28 William Turner Levy and Cynthia Eagle Russett, *The Extraordinary Mrs R: A Friend Remembers Eleanor Roosevelt* (New York, NY: John Wiley & Sons, 1999), p. 168.

CHAPTER 14

1 Quoted in *VOS*, p. 260.

2 Mackenzie King's account of this conversation can be found in *DMK*, pp. 687–89.

3 'Telegram from the King Expressing Thanks for Their Hospitality while in the United States', President Franklin D. Roosevelt Presidential Library and Museum [docs. fdrlibrary.marist.edu/telegram.html].

4 Quoted in the *Sydney Morning Herald*, 17th June 1939.

5 'Letter from FDR to the Royal Couple Showing His Appreciation for Their Visit', President Franklin D. Roosevelt Presidential Library and Museum (docs.fdr-library.marist.edu/bonvoyag.html).

6 Quoted in *VOS*, p. 308.

7 Quoted ibid., p. 309.

8 Ibid., p. 310.

9 Much of the following discussion of the King's Guildhall speech is derived from *KS*, pp. 155–56.

10 Ronald Lindsay to Lord Halifax, 20th June 1939 (*PRO FO* A4441/27/45).

11 *New York Times*, 10th June 1939; *New York Times*, 12th June 1939; *Washington Post*, 12th June 1939; *Christian Science Monitor*, 12th June 1939.

12 *Washington Star*, 8th June 1939.

13 Ronald Lindsay to Lord Halifax, 12th June 1939 (*PRO FO* A4139/2745).

14 Sir Godfrey Haggard to Ronald Lindsay, 14th June 1939, quoted in Fred M. Leventhal, 'Essential Democracy: The 1939 Visit to the United States', in George K. Behlmer and Fred M. Leventhal, eds., *Singular Continuities: Tradition, Nostalgia and Identity in Modern British Culture* (Stanford: Stanford University Press, 2000), p. 173.

15 *Time*, 19th June 1939.

16 *GVI:HLR*, p. 392.

CHAPTER 15

1 Quoted in Jean Edward Smith, *FDR* (New York, NY: Random House, 2007), p. 435.

2 *GVI:HLR*, p. 503.

3 Quoted in *GVI:HLR*, p. 510.

4 Quoted ibid., p. 511.

5 Quoted ibid., p. 513.

6 Quoted ibid., p. 525.

7 Quoted ibid., p. 533.

8 Quoted ibid., p. 550.

9 King George VI to President Roosevelt, 25th October 1942 (*PRO FO 954/29B/11555*).

10 *AER*, p. 240.

11 Quoted in *GVI:HLR*, p. 619.

12 Quoted in Doris Kearns Goodwin, *No Ordinary Time, Franklin and Eleanor Roosevelt: The Home Front in World War II* (New York, NY: Simon & Schuster, 1994), p. 568.

13 Quoted in *RR*, p. 263.
14 Quoted in the *New York Times*, 23rd October 1957.
15 *EAC*, p. 176.
16 *Time*, 18th November 1985; *New York Times*, 10th November 1985.

Index

Acknowledgements

The author and the publisher would like to thank Kirsten Strigel Carter and the Franklin D. Roosevelt Presidential Library & Museum for helping us source and letting us use the pictures from their library archive.

A special thank you goes to Library and Archives Canada and the US Library of Congress for making available the other pictures reproduced in this volume.